Contents

AWS Database Migration Service Step-by-Step Walkthroughs

You can use AWS Database Migration Service (AWS DMS) to migrate your data to and from most widely used commercial and open-source databases such as Oracle, PostgreSQL, Microsoft SQL Server, Amazon Redshift, Amazon Aurora, MariaDB, and MySQL. The service supports homogeneous migrations such as Oracle to Oracle, and also heterogeneous migrations between different database platforms, such as Oracle to MySQL or MySQL to Amazon Aurora with MySQL compatibility. The source or target database must be on an AWS service.

In this guide, you can find step-by-step walkthroughs that go through the process of migrating sample data to AWS:

- Migrating Databases to Amazon Web Services (AWS)
- Migrating an On-Premises Oracle Database to Amazon Aurora MySQL
- Migrating an Amazon RDS Oracle Database to Amazon Aurora MySQL
- Migrating a SQL Server Database to Amazon Aurora MySQL
- Migrating an Oracle Database to PostgreSQL
- Migrating an Amazon RDS for Oracle Database to Amazon Redshift
- Migrating MySQL-Compatible Databases to AWS
- Migrating a MySQL-Compatible Database to Amazon Aurora MySQL

AWS Database Migration Service Step-by-Step Migration Guide

A catalogue record for this book is available from the Hong Kong Public Libraries.

Published in Hong Kong by Samurai Media Limited.

Email: info@samuraimedia.org

ISBN 9789888408863

Contents

AWS Database Migration Service Step-by-Step Walkthroughs

You can use AWS Database Migration Service (AWS DMS) to migrate your data to and from most widely used commercial and open-source databases such as Oracle, PostgreSQL, Microsoft SQL Server, Amazon Redshift, Amazon Aurora, MariaDB, and MySQL. The service supports homogeneous migrations such as Oracle to Oracle, and also heterogeneous migrations between different database platforms, such as Oracle to MySQL or MySQL to Amazon Aurora with MySQL compatibility. The source or target database must be on an AWS service.

In this guide, you can find step-by-step walkthroughs that go through the process of migrating sample data to AWS:

- Migrating Databases to Amazon Web Services (AWS)
- Migrating an On-Premises Oracle Database to Amazon Aurora MySQL
- Migrating an Amazon RDS Oracle Database to Amazon Aurora MySQL
- Migrating a SQL Server Database to Amazon Aurora MySQL
- Migrating an Oracle Database to PostgreSQL
- Migrating an Amazon RDS for Oracle Database to Amazon Redshift
- Migrating MySQL-Compatible Databases to AWS
- Migrating a MySQL-Compatible Database to Amazon Aurora MySQL

Migrating Databases to Amazon Web Services (AWS)

AWS Migration Tools

You can use several AWS tools and services to migrate data from an external database to AWS. Depending on the type of database migration you are doing, you may find that the native migration tools for your database engine are also effective.

AWS Database Migration Service (AWS DMS) helps you migrate databases to AWS efficiently and securely. The source database can remain fully operational during the migration, minimizing downtime to applications that rely on the database. AWS DMS can migrate your Oracle data to the most widely used commercial and open-source databases on AWS.

AWS DMS migrates data, tables, and primary keys to the target database. All other database elements are not migrated. If you are migrating an Oracle database to Amazon Aurora with MySQL compatibility, for example, you would want to use the AWS Schema Conversion Tool in conjunction with AWS DMS.

The AWS Schema Conversion Tool (SCT) makes heterogeneous database migrations easy by automatically converting the source database schema and a majority of the custom code, including views, stored procedures, and functions, to a format compatible with the target database. Any code that cannot be automatically converted is clearly marked so that it can be manually converted. You can use this tool to convert your source Oracle databases to an Amazon Aurora MySQL, MySQL, or PostgreSQL target database on either Amazon RDS or EC2.

It is important to understand that DMS and SCT are two different tools and serve different needs and they don't interact with each other in the migration process. As per the DMS best practice, migration methodology for this tutorial is outlined as below:

- AWS DMS takes a minimalist approach and creates only those objects required to efficiently migrate the data for example tables with primary key – therefore, we will use DMS to load the tables with data without any foreign keys or constraints. (We can also use the SCT to generate the table scripts and create it on the target before performing the load via DMS).

- We will leverage SCT:

  - To identify the issues, limitations and actions for the schema conversion

  - To generate the target schema scripts including foreign key and constraints

  - To convert code such as procedures and views from source to target and apply it on target

The size and type of Oracle database migration you want to do greatly determines the tools you should use. For example, a heterogeneous migration, where you are migrating from an Oracle database to a different database engine on AWS, is best accomplished using AWS DMS. A homogeneous migration, where you are migrating from an Oracle database to an Oracle database on AWS, is best accomplished using native Oracle tools.

Walkthroughs in this Guide

Migrating an On-Premises Oracle Database to Amazon Aurora MySQL

Migrating an Amazon RDS Oracle Database to Amazon Aurora MySQL

Migrating a SQL Server Database to Amazon Aurora MySQL

Migrating an Oracle Database to PostgreSQL

Migrating an Amazon RDS for Oracle Database to Amazon Redshift

Migrating MySQL-Compatible Databases to AWS

Migrating a MySQL-Compatible Database to Amazon Aurora MySQL

Migrating an On-Premises Oracle Database to Amazon Aurora MySQL

Following, you can find a high-level outline and also a complete step-by-step walkthrough that both show the process for migrating an on-premises Oracle database (the source endpoint) to an Amazon Aurora with MySQL compatibility (the target endpoint) using AWS Database Migration Service (AWS DMS) and the AWS Schema Conversion Tool (AWS SCT).

AWS DMS migrates your data from your Oracle source into your Aurora MySQL target. AWS DMS also captures data manipulation language (DML) and data definition language (DDL) changes that happen on your source database and apply these changes to your target database. This way, AWS DMS helps keep your source and target databases in synch with each other. To facilitate the data migration, DMS creates tables and primary key indexes on the target database if necessary.

However, AWS DMS doesn't migrate your secondary indexes, sequences, default values, stored procedures, triggers, synonyms, views and other schema objects not specifically related to data migration. To migrate these objects to your Aurora MySQL target, use the AWS Schema Conversion Tool.

We highly recommend that you follow along using the Amazon sample database. To find a tutorial that uses the sample database and instructions on how to get a copy of the sample database, see Working with the Sample Database for Migration.

If you've used AWS DMS before or you prefer clicking a mouse to reading, you probably want to work with the high-level outline. If you need the details and want a more measured approach (or run into questions), you probably want the step-by-step guide.

Topic: Migration from On-Premises Oracle to Aurora MySQL or MySQL on Amazon RDS
Time:
Cost:
Source Database: Oracle
Target Database: Amazon Aurora MySQL/MySQL
Restrictions: Oracle Edition: Enterprise, Standard, Express and Personal **Oracle Version:** 10g (10.2 and later), 11g, 12c, (On Amazon Relational Database Service (Amazon RDS), 11g or higher is required.) **MySQL or Related Database Version:** 5.5, 5.6, 5.7, MariaDB, Amazon Aurora MySQL **Character Set:** utf8mb4 is not currently supported

Costs

Because AWS DMS isn't incorporated into the calculator yet, see the following table for a pricing estimate.

In addition to the setup on your own PC, you must create several AWS components to complete the migration process. The AWS components include:

AWS Service	Type	Description
Amazon Aurora MySQL DB instance	db.r3.large	Single AZ, 10 GB storage, 1 million I/O
AWS DMS replication instance	T2.large	50 GB of storage for keeping replication logs included
AWS DMS data transfer	Free, based on the amount of data transferred for the sample database.	
Data transfer out	First 1 GB per month free	

Migration High-Level Outline

To migrate your data from Oracle to Aurora MySQL using AWS DMS, you take the following steps. If you've used AWS DMS before or prefer clicking a mouse to reading, the following summary should help you kick-start your migration. To get the details about migration or if you run into questions, see the step-by-step guide.

Step 1: Prepare Your Oracle Source Database

To use AWS DMS to migrate data from an Oracle source database requires some preparation and we also recommend a few additional steps as best practices.

- AWS DMS account – It's a good practice to create a separate account for the specific purpose of migrating your data. This account should have the minimal set of privileges required to migrate your data. Specific details regarding those privileges are outlined below. If you are simply interested in testing AWS DMS on a non-production database, any DBA account will be sufficient.

- Supplemental logging – To capture changes, you must enable supplemental logging in order to use DMS. To enable supplemental logging at the database level issue the following command.

```
1 ALTER DATABASE ADD SUPPLEMENTAL LOG DATA
```

  Additionally, AWS DMS requires for each table being migrated, you set at least key-level supplemental logging. AWS DMS automatically adds this supplemental logging for you if you include the following extra connection parameter for your source connection.

```
1 addSupplementalLogging=Y
```

- Source database – To migrate your data, the AWS DMS replication server needs access to your source database. Make sure that your firewall rules give the AWS DMS replication server ingress.

Step 2: Launch and Prepare Your Aurora MySQL Target Database

Following are some things to consider when launching your Aurora MySQL instance:

- For best results, we recommend that you locate your Aurora MySQL instance and your replication instance in the same VPC and, if possible, the same Availability Zone.

- We recommend that you create a separate account with minimal privileges for migrating your data. The AWS DMS account needs the following privileges on all databases to which data is being migrated.

```
1 ALTER, CREATE, DROP, INDEX, INSERT, UPDATE, DELETE, SELECT
```

  Additionally, AWS DMS needs complete access to the awsdms_control database. This database holds information required by AWS DMS specific to the migration. To provide access, run the following command.

```
1 ALL PRIVILEGES ON awsdms_control.* TO 'dms_user'
```

Step 3: Launch a Replication Instance

The AWS DMS service connects to your source and target databases from a replication instance. Here are some things to consider when launching your replication instance:

- For best results, we recommend that you locate your replication instance in the same VPC and Availability Zone as your target database, in this case Aurora MySQL.

- If either your source or target database is outside of the VPC where you launch your replication server, the replication server must be publicly accessible.

- AWS DMS can consume a fair bit of memory and CPU. However, it's easy enough to scale up if necessary. If you anticipate running several tasks on a single replication server or

- The default storage is usually enough for most migrations.

Step 4: Create a Source Endpoint

For AWS DMS to access your Oracle source database you'll need to create a source endpoint. The source endpoint defines all the information required for AWS DMS to connect to your source database from the replication server. Following are some requirements for the source endpoint.

- Your source endpoint needs to be accessible from the replication server. To allow this, you will likely need to modify your firewall rules to whitelist the replication server. You can find the IP address of your replication server in the AWS DMS Management Console.

- For AWS DMS to capture changes, Oracle requires supplemental logging be enabled. If you want AWS DMS to enable supplemental logging for you, add the following to the extra connection attributes for your Oracle source endpoint.

```
1  addSupplementalLogging=Y
```

Step 5: Create a Target Endpoint

For AWS DMS to access your Aurora MySQL target database you'll need to create a target endpoint. The target endpoint defines all the information required for DMS to connect to your Aurora MySQL database.

- Your target endpoint needs to be accessible from the replication server. You might need to modify your security groups to make the target endpoint accessible.

- If you've pre-created the database on your target, it's a good idea to disable foreign key checks during the full load. To do so, add the following to your extra connection attributes.

```
1  initstmt=SET FOREIGN_KEY_CHECKS=0
```

Step 6: Create and Run a Migration Task

A migration task tells AWS DMS where and how you want your data migrated. When creating your migration task, you should consider setting migration parameters as follows.

Endpoints and replication server — Choose the endpoints and replication server created above.

Migration type — In most cases you'll want to choose **migrate existing data and replication ongoing changes**. With this option, AWS DMS loads your source data while capturing changes to that data. When the data is fully loaded, AWS DMS applies any outstanding changes and keeps the source and target databases in sync until the task is stopped.

Target table preparation mode ** — If you're having AWS DMS create your tables, **choose drop tables on target. If you're using some other method to create your target tables such as the AWS Schema Conversion Tool, choose **truncate.**

LOB parameters ** — If you're just trying AWS DMS, choose **include LOB columns in replication, Limited LOB mode, and set your **max LOB size to 16** (which is 16k.) For more information regarding LOBs, read the details in the step-by-step guide.

**Enable logging ** — To help with debugging migration issues, always enable logging.

**Table mappings ** — When migrating from Oracle to Aurora MySQL, we recommend that you convert your schema, table, and column names to lowercase. To do so, create a custom table mapping. The following example migrates the schema DMS_SAMPLE and converts schema, table and column names to lower case.

```
1  {
2    "rules": [
3      {
4        "rule-type": "selection",
5        "rule-id": "1",
6        "rule-name": "1",
7        "object-locator": {
8          "schema-name": "DMS_SAMPLE",
9          "table-name": "%"
10       },
11       "rule-action": "include"
12     },
13     {
14       "rule-type": "transformation",
15       "rule-id": "6",
16       "rule-name": "6",
17       "rule-action": "convert-lowercase",
18       "rule-target": "schema",
19       "object-locator": {
20         "schema-name": "%"
21       }
22     },
23     {
24       "rule-type": "transformation",
25       "rule-id": "7",
26       "rule-name": "7",
27       "rule-action": "convert-lowercase",
28       "rule-target": "table",
29       "object-locator": {
30         "schema-name": "%",
31         "table-name": "%"
32       }
33     },
34     {
35       "rule-type": "transformation",
36       "rule-id": "8",
37       "rule-name": "8",
38       "rule-action": "convert-lowercase",
39       "rule-target": "column",
40       "object-locator": {
41         "schema-name": "%",
42         "table-name": "%",
43         "column-name": "%"
44       }
45     }
46   ]
47 }
```

Migration Step-by-Step Guide

Following, you can find step-by-step instructions for migrating an Oracle database from an on-premises environment to Amazon Aurora MySQL. These instructions assume that you have already done the setting up steps for using AWS DMS located at Setting Up to Use AWS Database Migration Service.

- Step 1: Configure Your Oracle Source Database
- Step 2: Configure Your Aurora Target Database
- Step 3: Creating a Replication Instance
- Step 4: Create Your Oracle Source Endpoint
- Step 5: Create Your Aurora MySQL Target Endpoint
- Step 6: Create a Migration Task
- Step 7: Monitor Your Migration Task
- Troubleshooting

Step 1: Configure Your Oracle Source Database

To use Oracle as a source for AWS Database Migration Service (AWS DMS), you must first ensure that ARCHIVELOG MODE is on to provide information to LogMiner. AWS DMS uses LogMiner to read information from the archive logs so that AWS DMS can capture changes.

For AWS DMS to read this information, make sure the archive logs are retained on the database server as long as AWS DMS requires them. If you configure your task to begin capturing changes immediately, you should only need to retain archive logs for a little longer than the duration of the longest running transaction. Retaining archive logs for 24 hours is usually sufficient. If you configure your task to begin from a point in time in the past, archive logs need to be available from that time forward. For more specific instructions for enabling ARCHIVELOG MODE and ensuring log retention for your on-premises Oracle database see the Oracle documentation.

To capture change data, AWS DMS requires supplemental logging to be enabled on your source database for AWS DMS. Minimal supplemental logging must be enabled at the database level. AWS DMS also requires that identification key logging be enabled. This option causes the database to place all columns of a row's primary key in the redo log file whenever a row containing a primary key is updated (even if no value in the primary key has changed). You can set this option at the database or table level.

If your Oracle source is in Amazon RDS, your database will be placed in ARCHIVELOG MODE if, and only if, you enable backups. The following command will ensure archive logs are retained on your RDS source for 24 hours:

```
1 exec rdsadmin.rdsadmin_util.set_configuration('archivelog retention hours',24);
```

To configure your Oracle source database

1. Run the following command to enable supplemental logging at the database level, which AWS DMS requires:

```
1 ALTER DATABASE ADD SUPPLEMENTAL LOG DATA;
2
3 For RDS:
4 exec rdsadmin.rdsadmin_util.alter_supplemental_logging('ADD');
```

2. Use the following command to enable identification key supplemental logging at the database level. AWS DMS requires supplemental key logging at the database level unless you allow AWS DMS to automatically add supplemental logging as needed or enable key-level supplemental logging at the table level:

```
1 ALTER DATABASE ADD SUPPLEMENTAL LOG DATA (PRIMARY KEY) COLUMNS;
2
3 For RDS:
4 exec rdsadmin.rdsadmin_util.alter_supplemental_logging('ADD','PRIMARY KEY');
```

3. Your source database incurs a small bit of overhead when key level supplemental logging is enabled. Therefore, if you are migrating only a subset of your tables, you might want to enable key level supplemental logging at the table level. To enable key level supplemental logging at the table level, use the following command.

```
1 alter table table_name add supplemental log data (PRIMARY KEY) columns;
```

If a table does not have a primary key you have two options.

- You can add supplemental logging to all columns involved in the first unique index on the table (sorted by index name.)

- You can add supplemental logging on all columns of the table.

13

To add supplemental logging on a subset of columns in a table, that is those involved in a unique index, run the following command.

```
1 ALTER TABLE table_name ADD SUPPLEMENTAL LOG GROUP example_log_group (ID,NAME)
2 ALWAYS;
```

To add supplemental logging for all columns of a table, run the following command.

```
1 alter table table_name add supplemental log data (ALL) columns;
```

4. Create or configure a database account to be used by AWS DMS. We recommend that you use an account with the minimal privileges required by AWS DMS for your AWS DMS connection. AWS DMS requires the following privileges.

```
 1 CREATE SESSION
 2 SELECT ANY TRANSACTION
 3 SELECT on V_$ARCHIVED_LOG
 4 SELECT on V_$LOG
 5 SELECT on V_$LOGFILE
 6 SELECT on V_$DATABASE
 7 SELECT on V_$THREAD
 8 SELECT on V_$PARAMETER
 9 SELECT on V_$NLS_PARAMETERS
10 SELECT on V_$TIMEZONE_NAMES
11 SELECT on V_$TRANSACTION
12 SELECT on ALL_INDEXES
13 SELECT on ALL_OBJECTS
14 SELECT on ALL_TABLES
15 SELECT on ALL_USERS
16 SELECT on ALL_CATALOG
17 SELECT on ALL_CONSTRAINTS
18 SELECT on ALL_CONS_COLUMNS
19 SELECT on ALL_TAB_COLS
20 SELECT on ALL_IND_COLUMNS
21 SELECT on ALL_LOG_GROUPS
22 SELECT on SYS.DBA_REGISTRY
23 SELECT on SYS.OBJ$
24 SELECT on DBA_TABLESPACES
25 SELECT on ALL_TAB_PARTITIONS
26 SELECT on ALL_ENCRYPTED_COLUMNS
27 * SELECT on all tables migrated
```

If you want to capture and apply changes (CDC) you also need the following privileges.

```
1 EXECUTE on DBMS_LOGMNR
2 SELECT on V_$LOGMNR_LOGS
3 SELECT on V_$LOGMNR_CONTENTS
4 LOGMINING /* For Oracle 12c and higher. */
5 * ALTER for any table being replicated (if you want DMS to add supplemental logging)
```

For Oracle versions before 11.2.0.3, you need the following privileges. If views are exposed, you need the following privileges.

```
1 SELECT on DBA_OBJECTS /* versions before 11.2.0.3 */
2 SELECT on ALL_VIEWS (required if views are exposed)
```

Step 2: Configure Your Aurora Target Database

As with your source database, it's a good idea to restrict access of the user you're connecting with. You can also create a temporary user that you can remove after the migration.

```
1 CREATE USER 'dms_user'@'%' IDENTIFIED BY 'dms_user';
2 GRANT ALTER, CREATE, DROP, INDEX, INSERT, UPDATE, DELETE,
3 SELECT ON <target database(s)>.* TO 'dms_user'@'%';
```

AWS DMS uses some control tables on the target in the database awsdms_control. The following command ensures that your dms_user has the necessary access to the awsdms_control database:

```
1 GRANT ALL PRIVILEGES ON awsdms_control.* TO 'dms_user'@'%';
2 flush privileges;
```

Step 3: Creating a Replication Instance

An AWS DMS replication instance performs the actual data migration between source and target. The replication instance also caches the changes during the migration. How much CPU and memory capacity a replication instance has influences the overall time required for the migration. Use the following procedure to set the parameters for a replication instance.

To create an AWS DMS replication instance

1. Sign in to the AWS Management Console, and open the AWS DMS console at https://console.aws.amazon. com/dms/ and choose **Replication instances**. If you are signed in as an AWS Identity and Access Management (IAM) user, you must have the appropriate permissions to access AWS DMS. For more information on the permissions required, see IAM Permissions Needed to Use AWS DMS.

2. Choose **Create replication instance**.

3. On the **Create replication instance** page, specify your replication instance information as shown following.
   [See the AWS documentation website for more details]

4. In the **Advanced** section, set the following parameters, and then choose **Next**.
   [See the AWS documentation website for more details]

Step 4: Create Your Oracle Source Endpoint

While your replication instance is being created, you can specify the Oracle source endpoint using the AWS Management Console. However, you can only test connectivity after the replication instance has been created, because the replication instance is used to test the connection.

To specify source or target database endpoints using the AWS console

1. In the AWS DMS console, choose **Endpoints** on the navigation pane.

2. Choose **Create endpoint**. The **Create database endpoint page** appears, as shown following.

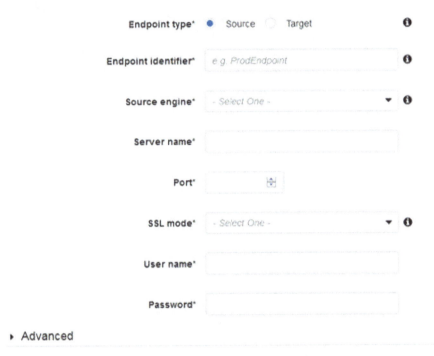

3. Specify your connection information for the source Oracle database. The following table describes the source settings.
   [See the AWS documentation website for more details]

4. Choose the **Advanced** tab to set values for extra connection strings and the encryption key.
   [See the AWS documentation website for more details]

Before you save your endpoint, you can test it. To do so, select a VPC and replication instance from which to perform the test. As part of the test AWS DMS refreshes the list of schemas associated with the endpoint. (The schemas are presented as source options when creating a task using this source endpoint.)

Step 5: Create Your Aurora MySQL Target Endpoint

Next, you can provide information for the target Amazon Aurora MySQL database by specifying the target endpoint settings. The following table describes the target settings.

To specify a target database endpoints using the AWS Management Console

1. In the AWS DMS console, choose **Endpoints** on the navigation pane.

2. Choose **Create endpoint**. The **Create database endpoint page** appears, as shown following.

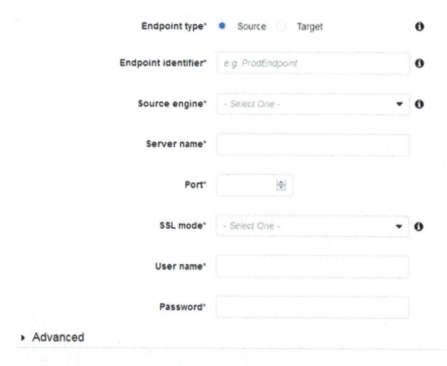

Create database endpoint

A database endpoint is used by the replication server to connect to a database. The database specified in the endpoint can be on-premise, on RDS, in EC2 or in the cloud. Details should be specified in the form below. It is recommended that you test your endpoint connections here to avoid errors during processing.

Endpoint type*	● Source ○ Target
Endpoint identifier*	e.g. ProdEndpoint
Source engine*	- Select One -
Server name*	
Port*	
SSL mode*	- Select One -
User name*	
Password*	

▸ Advanced

3. Specify your connection information for the target Aurora MySQL database. The following table describes the target settings.
   [See the AWS documentation website for more details]

4. Choose the **Advanced** tab to set values for extra connection strings and the encryption key if you need them.
   [See the AWS documentation website for more details]

Prior to saving your endpoint, you have an opportunity to test it. To do so you'll need to select a VPC and replication instance from which to perform the test.

Step 6: Create a Migration Task

When you create a migration task you tell AWS DMS exactly how you want your data migrated. Within a task you define which tables you'd like migrated, where you'd like them migrated, and how you'd like them migrated. If you're planning to use the change capture and apply capability of AWS DMS it's important to know transactions are maintained within a single task. In other words, you should migrate all tables that participate in a single transaction together in the same task.

Using an AWS DMS task, you can specify what schema to migrate and the type of migration. You can migrate existing data, migrate existing data and replicate ongoing changes, or replicate data changes only. This walkthrough migrates existing data only.

To create a migration task

1. On the navigation pane, choose **Tasks**.

2. Choose **Create Task**.

3. On the **Create Task** page, specify the task options. The following table describes the settings.
   [See the AWS documentation website for more details]

4. Next, set the Advanced settings as shown following.
   [See the AWS documentation website for more details]

5. Set additional parameters.
   [See the AWS documentation website for more details]

6. Specify any table mapping settings.

   Table mappings tell AWS DMS which tables a task should migrate from source to target. Table mappings are expressed in JSON, though some settings can be made using the AWS Management Console. Table mappings can also include transformations such as changing table names from upper case to lower case.

   AWS DMS generates default table mappings for each (non-system) schema in the source database. In most cases you'll want to customize your table mapping. To customize your table mapping select the custom radio button. For details on creating table mappings see the AWS DMS documentation. The following table mapping does these things:

   - It includes the DMS_SAMPLE schema in the migration.

   - It excludes the tables NFL_DATA, MLB_DATA, NAME_DATE, and STADIUM_DATA.

   - It converts the schema, table, and column names to lower case.

```
 1  {
 2    "rules": [
 3      {
 4        "rule-type": "selection",
 5        "rule-id": "1",
 6        "rule-name": "1",
 7        "object-locator": {
 8          "schema-name": "DMS_SAMPLE",
 9          "table-name": "%"
10        },
11        "rule-action": "include"
12      },
13
14      {
15        "rule-type": "selection",
16        "rule-id": "2",
17        "rule-name": "2",
```

```
18        "object-locator": {
19          "schema-name": "DMS_SAMPLE",
20          "table-name": "MLB_DATA"
21        },
22        "rule-action": "exclude"
23      },
24  {
25        "rule-type": "selection",
26        "rule-id": "3",
27        "rule-name": "3",
28        "object-locator": {
29          "schema-name": "DMS_SAMPLE",
30          "table-name": "NAME_DATA"
31        },
32        "rule-action": "exclude"
33      },
34
35      {
36        "rule-type": "selection",
37        "rule-id": "4",
38        "rule-name": "4",
39        "object-locator": {
40          "schema-name": "DMS_SAMPLE",
41          "table-name": "NFL_DATA"
42        },
43        "rule-action": "exclude"
44      },
45
46      {
47        "rule-type": "selection",
48        "rule-id": "5",
49        "rule-name": "5",
50        "object-locator": {
51          "schema-name": "DMS_SAMPLE",
52          "table-name": "NFL_STADIUM_DATA"
53        },
54        "rule-action": "exclude"
55      },{
56        "rule-type": "transformation",
57        "rule-id": "6",
58        "rule-name": "6",
59        "rule-action": "convert-lowercase",
60        "rule-target": "schema",
61        "object-locator": {
62          "schema-name": "%"
63        }
64      },
65      {
66        "rule-type": "transformation",
67        "rule-id": "7",
68        "rule-name": "7",
69        "rule-action": "convert-lowercase",
70        "rule-target": "table",
71        "object-locator": {
```

```
          "schema-name": "%",
          "table-name": "%"
        }
      },
      {
        "rule-type": "transformation",
        "rule-id": "8",
        "rule-name": "8",
        "rule-action": "convert-lowercase",
        "rule-target": "column",
        "object-locator": {
          "schema-name": "%",
          "table-name": "%",
          "column-name": "%"
        }
      }
    ]
}
```

Step 7: Monitor Your Migration Task

Three sections in the console provide visibility into what your migration task is doing:

- Task monitoring – The **Task Monitoring** tab provides insight into your full load throughput and also your change capture and apply latencies.

- Table statistics – The **Table Statistics** tab provides detailed information on the number of rows processed, type and number of transactions processed, and also information on DDL operations.

- Logs – From the **Logs** tab you can view your task's log file, (assuming you turned logging on.) If for some reason your task fails, search this file for errors. Additionally, you can look in the file for any warnings. Any data truncation in your task appears as a warning in the log file. If you need to, you can increase the logging level by using the AWS Command Line Interface (CLI).

Troubleshooting

The two most common problem areas when working with Oracle as a source and PostgreSQL as a target are: supplemental logging and case sensitivity.

- Supplemental logging – With Oracle, in order to replicate change data, supplemental logging must be enabled. However, if you enable supplemental logging at the database level, it sometimes still needs to be enabled when new tables are created. The best remedy for this is to allow AWS DMS to enable supplemental logging for you by using the extra connection attribute:

```
1  addSupplementalLogging=Y
```

- Case sensitivity: Oracle is case-insensitive (unless you use quotes around your object names). However, text appears in uppercase. Thus, AWS DMS defaults to naming your target objects in uppercase. In most cases, you'll want to use transformations to change schema, table, and column names to lower case.

For more tips, see the AWS DMS troubleshooting section in the AWS DMS User Guide.

To troubleshoot issues specific to Oracle, see the Oracle troubleshooting section:

Troubleshooting Oracle Specific Issues

To troubleshoot PostgreSQL issues, see the PostgreSQL troubleshooting section:

Troubleshooting PostgreSQL Specific Issues

Working with the Sample Database for Migration

We recommend working through the preceding outline and guide by using the sample Oracle database provided by Amazon. This database mimics a simple sporting event ticketing system. The scripts to generate the sample database are part of the .tar file located here: https://github.com/awslabs/aws-database-migration-samples.

To build the sample database, extract the .tar file and follow the instructions in the README and install files.

The sample includes approximately 8-10 GB of data. The sample database also includes the ticketManagment package, which you can use to generate some transactions. To generate transactions, log into SQL*Plus or SQL Developer and run the following as *dms_sample*:

```
1 SQL>exec  ticketManagement.generateTicketActivity(0.01,1000);
```

The first parameter is the transaction delay in seconds, the second is the number of transactions to generate. The procedure preceding simply "sells tickets" to people. You'll see updates to the tables: sporting_event_ticket, and ticket_purchase_history.

Once you've "sold" some tickets, you can transfer them using the command following:

```
1 SQL>exec ticketManagement.generateTransferActivity(1,100);
```

The first parameter is the transaction delay in seconds, the second is the number of transactions to generate. This procedure also updates sporting_event_ticket and ticket_purchase_history.

Migrating an Amazon RDS Oracle Database to Amazon Aurora MySQL

This walkthrough gets you started with heterogeneous database migration from Amazon RDS Oracle to Amazon Aurora with MySQL compatibility using AWS Database Migration Service and the AWS Schema Conversion Tool. This is an introductory exercise so does not cover all scenarios but will provide you with a good understanding of the steps involved in executing such a migration.

It is important to understand that AWS DMS and AWS SCT are two different tools and serve different needs. They don't interact with each other in the migration process. At a high level, the steps involved in this migration are:

1. Using the AWS SCT to:

- Run the conversion report for Oracle to Aurora MySQL to identify the issues, limitations, and actions required for the schema conversion.

- Generate the schema scripts and apply them on the target before performing the data load via AWS DMS. AWS SCT will perform the necessary code conversion for objects like procedures and views.

1. Identify and implement solutions to the issues reported by AWS SCT. For example, an object type like Oracle Sequence that is not supported in the Amazon Aurora MySQL can be handled using the auto_increment option to populate surrogate keys or develop logic for sequences at the application layer.

2. Disable foreign keys or any other constraints which may impact the AWS DMS data load.

3. AWS DMS loads the data from source to target using the Full Load approach. Although AWS DMS is capable of creating objects in the target as part of the load, it follows a minimalistic approach to efficiently migrate the data so it doesn't copy the entire schema structure from source to target.

4. Perform post-migration activities such as creating additional indexes, enabling foreign keys, and making the necessary changes in the application to point to the new database.

This walkthrough uses a custom AWS CloudFormation template to create an Amazon RDS DB instances for Oracle and Amazon Aurora MySQL. It then uses a SQL command script to install a sample schema and data onto the Amazon RDS Oracle DB instance that you then migrate to Amazon Aurora MySQL.

This walkthrough takes approximately two hours to complete. The estimated cost to complete it, using AWS resources, is about $5.00. Be sure to follow the instructions to delete resources at the end of this walkthrough to avoid additional charges.

- Costs
- Prerequisites
- Migration Architecture
- Step-by-Step Migration
- Next Steps
- AWS CloudFormation Template, SQL Scripts, and Other Resources
- References

Costs

For this walkthrough, you provision Amazon Relational Database Service (Amazon RDS) resources by using AWS CloudFormation and also AWS Database Migration Service (AWS DMS) resources. Provisioning these resources will incur charges to your AWS account by the hour. The AWS Schema Conversion Tool incurs no cost; it is provided as a part of AWS DMS.

Although you'll need only a minimum of resources for this walkthrough, some of these resources are not eligible for AWS Free Tier. At the end of this walkthrough, you'll find a section in which you delete the resources to avoid additional charges. Delete the resources as soon as you complete the walkthrough.

To estimate what it will cost to run this walkthrough on AWS, you can use the AWS Simple Monthly Calculator. However, the AWS DMS service is not incorporated into the calculator yet. The following table shows both AWS DMS and Amazon RDS Oracle Standard Edition Two pricing.

AWS Service	Instance Type	Storage and I/O
Amazon RDS Oracle DB instance, License Included (Standard Edition Two), Single AZ	db.m3.medium	Single AZ, 10 GB storage, GP2
Amazon Aurora MySQL DB instance	db.r3.large	Single AZ, 10 GB storage, 1 million I/O
AWS DMS replication instance	t2.small	50 GB of storage for keeping replication logs included
AWS DMS data transfer	Free—data transfer between AWS DMS and databases in RDS instances in the same Availability Zone is free	
Data transfer out	First 1 GB per month free	

Assuming you run this walkthrough for two hours, we estimate the following pricing for AWS resources:

- Amazon Aurora MySQL + 10 GB storage pricing estimated by using the AWS Simple Monthly Calculator is $1.78.

- Amazon RDS Oracle SE2 (license included) + 10 GB GP2 storage cost, estimated as per the pricing site at ($0.226) * 2 hours + ($0.115) * 10 GB, is $1.602.

- AWS DMS service cost for the t2.small instance with 50 GB GP2 storage, estimated as per the pricing site at ($0.036) * 2 hours, is $0.072.

Total estimated cost to run this project = $1.78 + $1.602 + $0.072 = $3.454—approximately $5.00.

This pricing is based on the following assumptions:

- We assume the total data transfer to the Internet is less than a gigabyte. The preceding pricing estimate assumes that data transfer and backup charges associated with the RDS and DMS services are within Free Tier limits.

- Storage consumed by the Aurora MySQL database is billed in per GB-month increments, and I/Os consumed are billed in per-million request increments.

- Data transfer between DMS and databases in RDS instances in the same Availability Zone is free.

Prerequisites

The following prerequisites are also required to complete this walkthrough:

- Familiarity with Amazon RDS, Amazon Redshift, the applicable database technologies, and SQL.

- The custom scripts that include creating the tables to be migrated and SQL queries for confirming the migration, as listed following:

  - SQL statements to build the SH schema

  - AWS CloudFormation template

  Each step in the walkthrough also contains a link to download the file involved or includes the exact query in the step.

- An AWS account with AWS Identity and Access Management (IAM) credentials that allow you to launch RDS, AWS Database Migration Service (AWS DMS) instances, and Amazon Redshift clusters in your AWS Region. For information about IAM credentials, see Creating an IAM User.

- Basic knowledge of the Amazon Virtual Private Cloud (Amazon VPC) service and of security groups. For information about using Amazon VPC with Amazon RDS, see Virtual Private Clouds (VPCs) and Amazon RDS. For information about Amazon RDS security groups, see Amazon RDS Security Groups. For information about using Amazon Redshift in a VPC, see Managing Clusters in an Amazon Virtual Private Cloud (VPC).

- An understanding of the supported features and limitations of AWS DMS. For information about AWS DMS, see What Is AWS Database Migration Service?

- Knowledge of the supported data type conversion options for Oracle and Amazon Redshift. For information about data types for Oracle as a source, see Using an Oracle Database as a Source for AWS Database Migration Service. For information about data types for Amazon Redshift as a target, see Using an Amazon Redshift Database as a Target for AWS Database Migration Service .

For more information about AWS DMS, see the AWS DMS documentation.

Migration Architecture

This walkthrough uses AWS CloudFormation to create a simple network topology for database migration that includes the source database, the replication instance, and the target database in the same VPC. For more information on AWS CloudFormation, see the CloudFormation documentation.

We provision the AWS resources that are required for this AWS DMS walkthrough through AWS CloudFormation. These resources include a VPC and Amazon RDS instance for Oracle and an Amazon Redshift cluster. We provision through CloudFormation because it simplifies the process, so we can concentrate on tasks related to data migration. When you create a stack from the CloudFormation template, it provisions the following resources:

- A VPC with CIDR (10.0.0.0/24) with two public subnets in your region, DBSubnet1 at the address 10.0.0.0/26 in Availability Zone (AZ) 1 and DBSubnet2 at the address 10.0.0.64/26, in AZ 12.

- A DB subnet group that includes DBSubnet1 and DBSubnet2.

- Oracle RDS Standard Edition Two with these deployment options:
  - License Included
  - Single-AZ setup
  - db.m3.medium or equivalent instance class
  - Port 1521
  - Default option and parameter groups

- Amazon Redshift cluster with these deployment options:
  - dc1.large
  - Port 5439
  - Default parameter group

- A security group with ingress access from your computer or 0.0.0.0/0 (access from anywhere) based on the input parameter

We have designed the CloudFormation template to require few inputs from the user. It provisions the necessary AWS resources with minimum recommended configurations. However, if you want to change some of the configurations and parameters, such as the VPC CIDR block and Amazon RDS instance types, feel free to update the template.

We use the AWS Management Console to provision the AWS DMS resources, such as the replication instance, endpoints, and tasks. You install client tools such as SQL Workbench/J and the AWS Schema Conversion Tool (AWS SCT) on your local computer to connect to the Amazon RDS instances.

Following is an illustration of the migration architecture for this walkthrough.

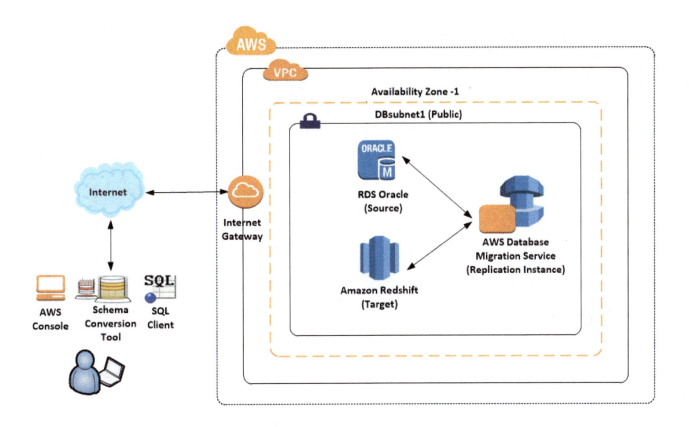

Step-by-Step Migration

In the following sections, you can find step-by-step instructions for migrating an Amazon RDS for Oracle database to Amazon Redshift. These steps assume that you have already prepared your source database as described in preceding sections.

- Step 1: Launch the RDS Instances in a VPC by Using the CloudFormation Template
- Step 2: Install the SQL Tools and AWS Schema Conversion Tool on Your Local Computer
- Step 3: Test Connectivity to the Oracle DB Instance and Create the Sample Schema
- Step 4: Test the Connectivity to the Amazon Redshift Database
- Step 5: Use AWS SCT to Convert the Oracle Schema to Amazon Redshift
- Step 6: Validate the Schema Conversion
- Step 7: Create an AWS DMS Replication Instance
- Step 8: Create AWS DMS Source and Target Endpoints
- Step 9: Create and Run Your AWS DMS Migration Task
- Step 10: Verify That Your Data Migration Completed Successfully
- Step 11: Delete Walkthrough Resources

Step 1: Launch the RDS Instances in a VPC by Using the CloudFormation Template

First, you need to provision the necessary AWS resources for this walkthrough.

To use AWS CloudFormation to create Amazon RDS resources for this walkthrough

1. Sign in to the AWS Management Console and open the AWS CloudFormation console at https://console.aws.amazon.com/cloudformation.

2. Choose **Create New Stack**.

3. On the **Select Template **page, choose **Specify an Amazon S3 template URL **and paste the following URL into the adjacent text box:

   https://dms/-sbs/.s3/.amazonaws/.com/Oracle/_Redshift/_For/_DMSDemo/.template

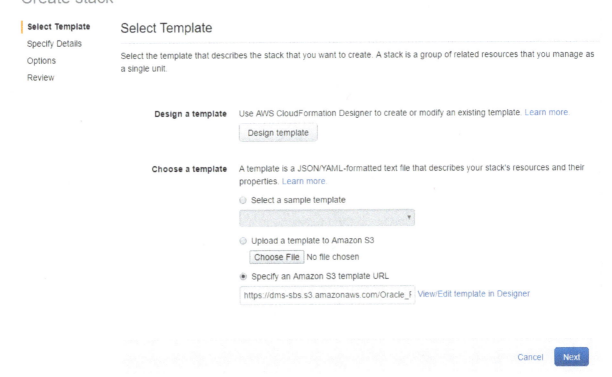

4. Choose **Next**. On the **Specify Details** page, provide parameter values as shown following. [See the AWS documentation website for more details]

31

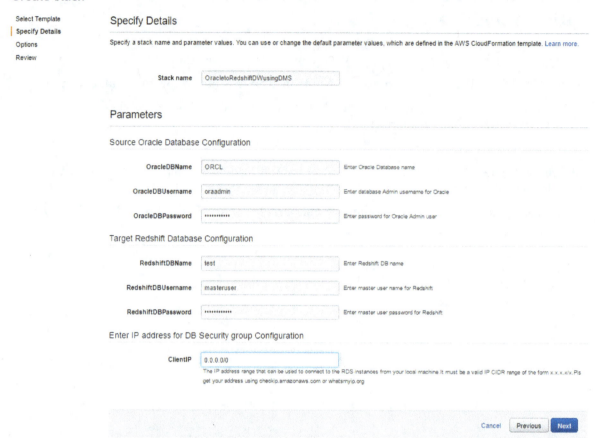

Create stack

Select Template
Specify Details
Options
Review

Specify Details

Specify a stack name and parameter values. You can use or change the default parameter values, which are defined in the AWS CloudFormation template. Learn more.

Stack name | OracletoRedshiftDWusingDMS

Parameters

Source Oracle Database Configuration

OracleDBName | ORCL | Enter Oracle Database name

OracleDBUsername | oraadmin | Enter database Admin username for Oracle

OracleDBPassword | ••••••••••• | Enter password for Oracle Admin user

Target Redshift Database Configuration

RedshiftDBName | test | Enter Redshift DB name

RedshiftDBUsername | masteruser | Enter master user name for Redshift

RedshiftDBPassword | ••••••••••• | Enter master user password for Redshift

Enter IP address for DB Security group Configuration

ClientIP | 0.0.0.0/0

The IP address range that can be used to connect to the RDS instances from your local machine. It must be a valid IP CIDR range of the form x.x.x.x/x. Pls get your address using checkip.amazonaws.com or whatsmyip.org

Cancel   Previous   **Next**

5. Choose **Next**. On the **Options** page, choose **Next**.

6. On the **Review** page, review the details, and if they are correct choose **Create**.

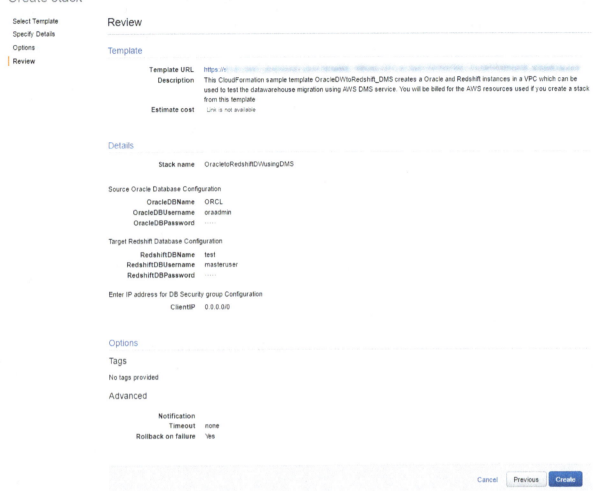

Create stack

Select Template
Specify Details
Options
Review

Review

Template

Template URL   https://...

Description   This CloudFormation sample template OracleDWtoRedshift_DMS creates a Oracle and Redshift instances in a VPC which can be used to test the datawarehouse migration using AWS DMS service. You will be billed for the AWS resources used if you create a stack from this template

Estimate cost   Link is not available

Details

Stack name   OracletoRedshiftDWusingDMS

Source Oracle Database Configuration

OracleDBName   ORCL
OracleDBUsername   oraadmin
OracleDBPassword   .....

Target Redshift Database Configuration

RedshiftDBName   test
RedshiftDBUsername   masteruser
RedshiftDBPassword   .....

Enter IP address for DB Security group Configuration

ClientIP   0.0.0.0/0

Options

Tags

No tags provided

Advanced

Notification
Timeout   none
Rollback on failure   Yes

Cancel   Previous   Create

7. AWS can take about 20 minutes or more to create the stack with an Amazon RDS Oracle instance and an Amazon Redshift cluster.

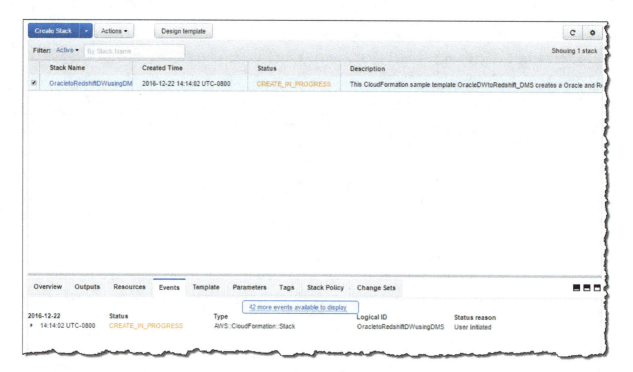

8. After the stack is created, select the **OracletoRedshiftDWusingDMS** stack, and then choose the **Outputs** view. Record the JDBC connection strings, **OracleJDBCConnectionString** and **RedshiftJDBCConnectionString**, for use later in this walkthrough to connect to the Oracle and Amazon Redshift databases.

Step 2: Install the SQL Tools and AWS Schema Conversion Tool on Your Local Computer

Next, you need to install a SQL client and AWS SCT on your local computer.

This walkthrough assumes you will use the SQL Workbench/J client to connect to the RDS instances for migration validation.

To install the SQL client software

1. Download SQL Workbench/J from the SQL Workbench/J website, and then install it on your local computer. This SQL client is free, open-source, and DBMS-independent.

2. Download the Oracle Database 12.1.0.2 JDBC driver (ojdbc7.jar).

3. Download the Amazon Redshift driver (RedshiftJDBC41-1.1.17.1017.jar).

4. Using SQL Workbench/J, configure JDBC drivers for Oracle and Amazon Redshift to set up connectivity, as described following.

   1. In SQL Workbench/J, choose **File**, then choose **Manage Drivers**.

   2. From the list of drivers, choose **Oracle**.

   3. Choose the **Open** icon, then choose the **ojdbc.jar** file that you downloaded in the previous step. Choose **OK**.

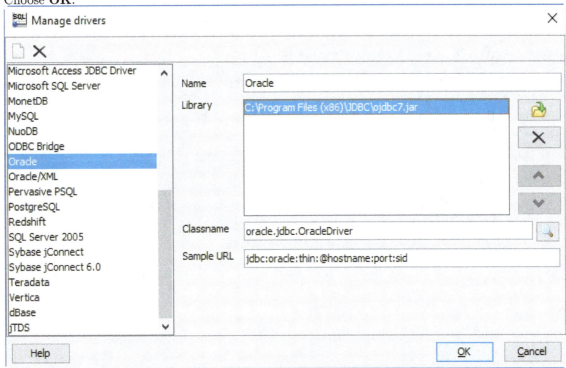

   4. From the list of drivers, choose **Redshift**.

   5. Choose the **Open** icon, then choose the Amazon Redshift JDBC driver that you downloaded in the previous step. Choose **OK**.

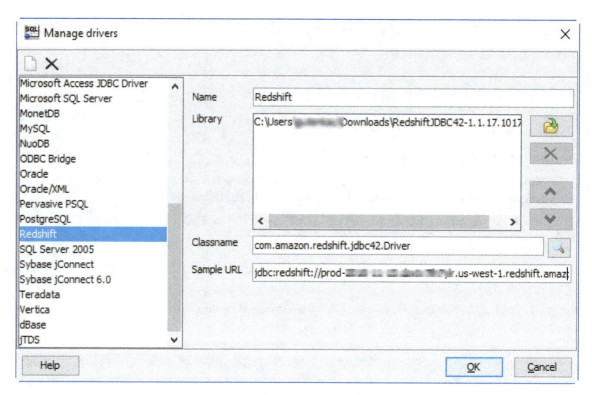

Next, install AWS SCT and the required JDBC drivers.

To install AWS SCT and the required JDBC drivers

1. Download AWS SCT from Installing and Updating the AWS Schema Conversion Tool in the *AWS Schema Conversion Tool User Guide.*

2. Follow the instructions to install AWS SCT. By default, the tool is installed in the `C:\Program Files\ AWS Schema Conversion Tool\AWS` directory.

3. Launch AWS SCT.

4. In AWS SCT, choose **Global Settings** from **Settings**.

5. Choose **Settings**, **Global Settings**, then choose **Drivers**, and then choose **Browse** for **Oracle Driver Path**. Locate the Oracle JDBC driver and choose **OK**.

6. Choose **Browse** for **Amazon Redshift Driver Path**. Locate the Amazon Redshift JDBC driver and choose **OK**. Choose **OK** to close the dialog box.

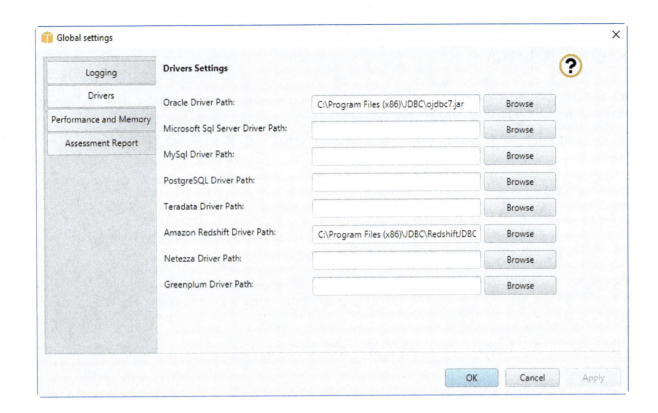

Step 3: Test Connectivity to the Oracle DB Instance and Create the Sample Schema

After the CloudFormation stack has been created, test the connection to the Oracle DB instance by using SQL Workbench/J and then create the HR sample schema.

To test the connection to your Oracle DB instance using SQL Workbench/J and create the sample schema

1. In SQL Workbench/J, choose **File**, then choose **Connect window**. Create a new connection profile using the following information.
   [See the AWS documentation website for more details]

2. Test the connection by choosing **Test**. Choose **OK** to close the dialog box, then choose **OK** to create the connection profile.

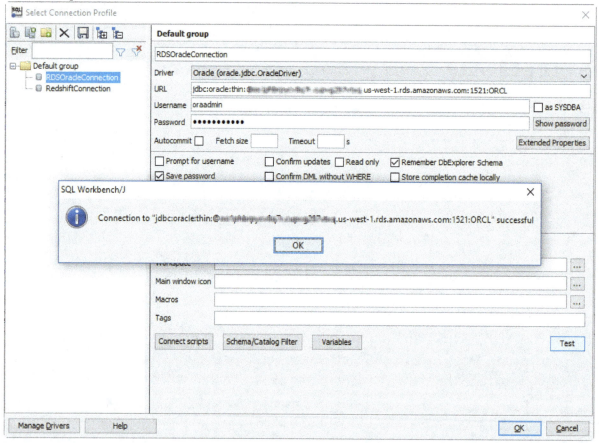

Note

If your connection is unsuccessful, ensure that the IP address you assigned when creating the CloudFormation template is the one you are attempting to connect from. This issue is the most common one when trying to connect to an instance.

3. Create the SH schema you will use for migration using a custom script. The SQL script provided by AWS is located https://dms-sbs.s3.amazonaws.com/Oraclesalesstarschema.sql.

   1. Open the provided SQL script in a text editor. Copy the entire script.

   2. In SQL Workbench/J, paste the SQL script in the Default.wksp window showing **Statement 1**.

   3. Choose **SQL**, then choose **Execute All**.

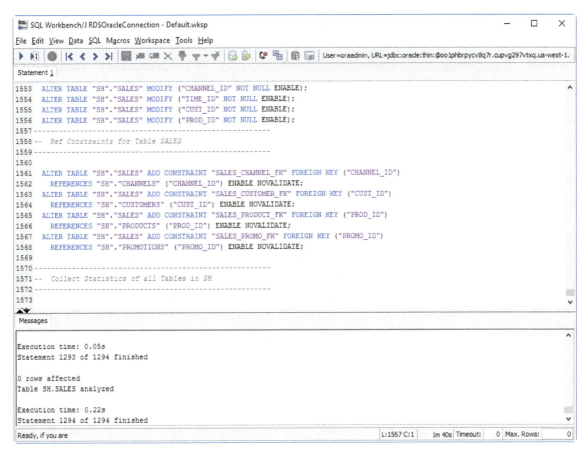

4. Verify the object types and count in SH Schema were created successfully by running the following SQL query.

```
1 Select OBJECT_TYPE, COUNT(*) from dba_OBJECTS where owner='SH'
2 GROUP BY OBJECT_TYPE;
```

The results of this query should be similar to the following.

```
1 OBJECT_TYPE      | COUNT(*)
2 ----------------+----------
3 INDEX PARTITION  |     40
4 TABLE PARTITION  |      8
5 TABLE            |      5
6 INDEX            |     15
```

5. Verify the total number of tables and number of rows for each table by running the following SQL query.

```
1 Select table_name, num_rows from dba_tables where owner='SH'  order by 1;
```

The results of this query should be similar to the following.

```
1 TABLE_NAME | NUM_ROWS
2 ----------+----------
3 CHANNELS   |      5
4 CUSTOMERS  |      8
5 PRODUCTS   |     66
6 PROMOTIONS |    503
7 SALES      |    553
```

6. Verify the integrity in tables. Check the number of sales made in different channels by running the following SQL query.

```
1 Select b.channel_desc,count(*) from SH.SALES a,SH.CHANNELS b where a.channel_id=b.
    channel_id
2 group by b.channel_desc
3 order by 1;
```

The results of this query should be similar to the following.

```
1 CHANNEL_DESC | COUNT(*)
2 -------------+----------
3 Direct Sales |     710
4 Internet     |      52
5 Partners     |     344
```

Note
The preceding examples are representative of validation queries. When you perform actual migrations, you should develop similar queries to validate the schema and the data integrity.

Step 4: Test the Connectivity to the Aurora MySQL DB Instance

Next, test your connection to your Aurora MySQL DB instance.

To test the connection to your Aurora MySQL DB instance using SQL Workbench/J

1. In SQL Workbench/J, choose **File**, then choose **Connect window**. Choose the Create a new connection profile icon. using the following information: Connect to the Aurora MySQL DB instance in SQL Workbench/J by using the information as shown following
   [See the AWS documentation website for more details]

2. Test the connection by choosing **Test**. Choose **OK** to close the dialog box, then choose OK to create the connection profile.

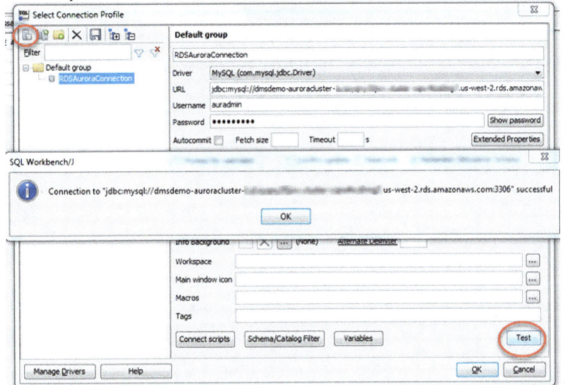

Note

If your connection is unsuccessful, ensure that the IP address you assigned when creating the CloudFormation template is the one you are attempting to connect from. This is the most common issue when trying to connect to an instance.

3. Log on to the Aurora MySQL instance by using the master admin credentials.

4. Verify your connectivity to the Aurora MySQL DB instance by running a sample SQL command, such as `SHOW DATABASES;`.

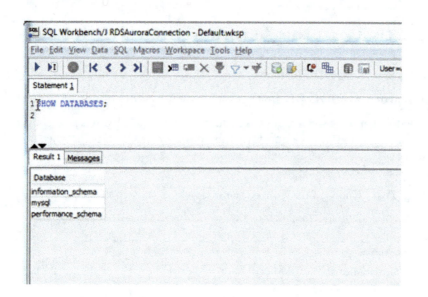

Step 5: Use the AWS Schema Conversion Tool (AWS SCT) to Convert the Oracle Schema to Aurora MySQL

Before you migrate data to Aurora MySQL, you convert the Oracle schema to an Aurora MySQL schema as described following.

To convert an Oracle schema to an Aurora MySQL schema using AWS Schema Conversion Tool (AWS SCT)

1. Launch the AWS Schema Conversion Tool (AWS SCT). In the AWS SCT, choose **File**, then choose **New Project**. Create a new project called **DMSDemoProject**. Enter the following information in the New Project window and then choose **OK**.
   [See the AWS documentation website for more details]

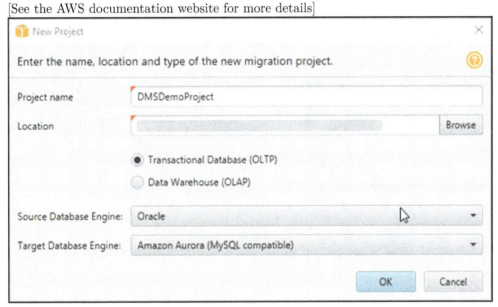

2. Choose **Connect to Oracle**. In the **Connect to Oracle** dialog box, enter the following information, and then choose **Test Connection**.
   [See the AWS documentation website for more details]

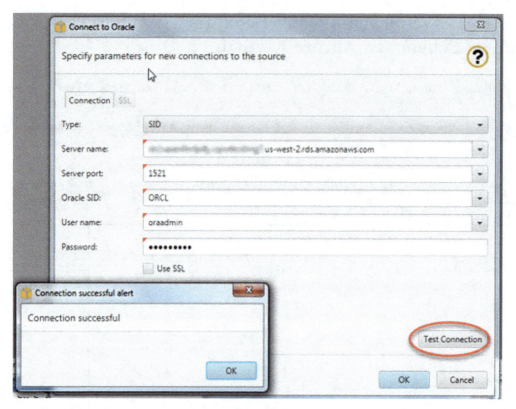

3. Choose **OK** to close the alert box, then choose OK to close the dialog box and to start the connection to the Oracle DB instance. The database structure on the Oracle DB instance is shown. Select only the HR schema.

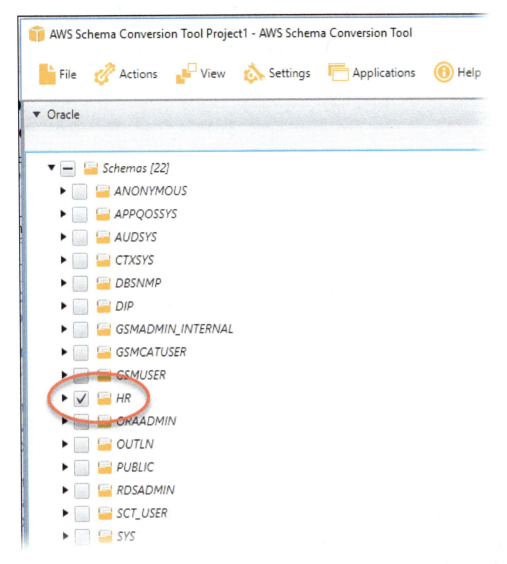

4. Choose **Connect to Amazon Aurora**. In the **Connect to Amazon Aurora** dialog box, enter the following information and then choose **Test Connection**.
[See the AWS documentation website for more details]

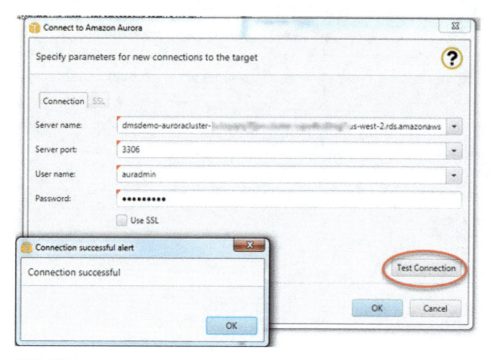

AWS SCT analyses the HR schema and creates a database migration assessment report for the conversion to Amazon Aurora MySQL.

5. Choose **OK** to close the alert box, then choose **OK** to close the dialog box to start the connection to the Amazon Aurora MySQL DB instance.

6. Right-click the HR schema and select **Create Report**.

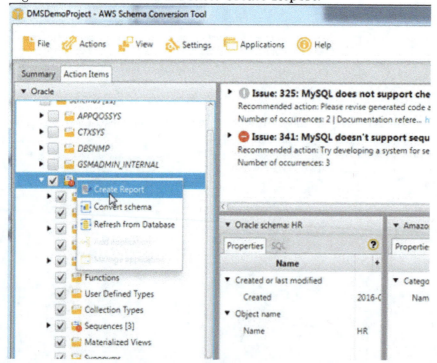

7. Check the report and the action items it suggests. The report discusses the type of objects that can be converted by using AWS SCT, along with potential migration issues and actions to resolve these issues. For this walkthrough, you should see something like the following.

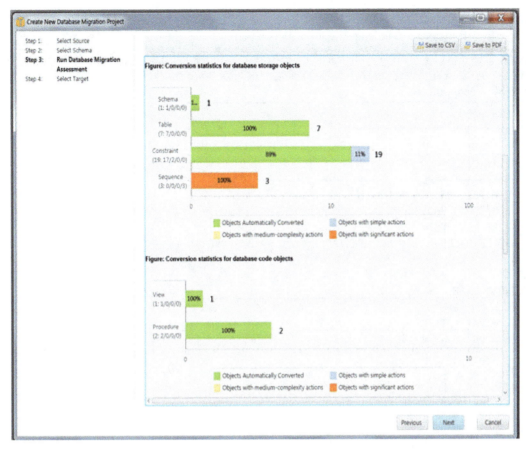

Figure: Conversion statistics for database storage objects

Figure: Conversion statistics for database code objects

8. Save the report as .csv or .pdf format for detailed analysis, and then choose the **Action Items** tab. In the action items, you will see two issues: 1. MySQL does not support Check constraints and 2. MySQL does not support Sequences.

Regarding action item #1, SCT automatically provisions triggers to simulate check constraints in Aurora MySQL database (Emulating triggers). For example, a check constraint for SAL > 0 in the EMPLOYEES table (in Oracle) is enforced with the help of before and update trigger statements in Aurora MySQL. If you would like to have this logic handled at the application layer, then you can drop or update the triggers if required.

Regarding action item #2, there are three sequence objects in the source database that are used to generate primary keys for the EMPLOYEES (EMPLOYEE_ID), DEPARTMENTS (DEPARTMENT_ID), LOCATIONS (LOCATION_ID) tables. As mentioned earlier in this walkthrough, one alternative to using sequences for Surrogate keys in Aurora MySQL is using the auto_increment feature. To enable the auto_increment feature, you must change the settings for SCT. For brevity, the following substeps show enabling auto_increment for EMPLOYEE_ID column in the EMPLOYEES table only. The same procedure can be repeated for the other sequence objects.

Before starting, please note enabling the auto_increment option requires some additional steps via SCT due to the below reasons:

- SCT by default converts all NUMBER (Oracle) data types into DECIMAL in Aurora MySQL (http://docs.aws.amazon.com/dms/latest/userguide/SchemaConversionTool/latest/user-guide/CHAP_SchemaConversionTool.Reference.ConversionSupport.Oracle.html#d0e50104).

- Aurora MySQL doesn't support auto_increment for the DECIMAL data type. Therefore, the data type of the primary key column and corresponding foreign key columns needs to be changed to one of the INTEGER data types such as INT, SMALLINT, MEDIUMINT or BIGINT as part of the schema conversion.

The good news is that the latest release of SCT provides a **Mapping Rules** feature that can be used to achieve the above transformation using the following steps:

1. For the EMPLOYEES table, you must identify the primary key and foreign key relationships by running the following query on the source Oracle database. Note the columns that need to be specified in the SCT Mapping rules.

```
1  SELECT * FROM
2  (SELECT
3   PK.TABLE_NAME,
4   C.COLUMN_NAME,
5   PK.CONSTRAINT_TYPE
6      FROM DBA_CONSTRAINTS PK,
7       DBA_CONS_COLUMNS C
8       WHERE PK.CONSTRAINT_NAME = C.CONSTRAINT_NAME
9       AND PK.OWNER = 'HR' AND PK.TABLE_NAME = 'EMPLOYEES' AND PK.CONSTRAINT_TYPE = 'P'
10 UNION
11   SELECT
12   FK.TABLE_NAME,
13   COL.COLUMN_NAME,
14   FK.CONSTRAINT_TYPE
15      FROM DBA_CONSTRAINTS PK,
16       DBA_CONSTRAINTS FK,
17       DBA_CONS_COLUMNS COL
18       WHERE PK.CONSTRAINT_NAME = FK.R_CONSTRAINT_NAME
19        AND FK.CONSTRAINT_TYPE = 'R'
20        AND FK.CONSTRAINT_NAME = COL.CONSTRAINT_NAME
21     AND PK.OWNER = 'HR' AND PK.TABLE_NAME = 'EMPLOYEES' AND PK.CONSTRAINT_TYPE = 'P' )
22     ORDER BY 3 ASC;
```

The results of the query should be similar to the following:

```
1  TABLE_NAME     COLUMN_NAME CONSTRAINT_TYPE
2  EMPLOYEES EMPLOYEE_ID P
3  JOB_HISTORY    EMPLOYEE_ID R
4  EMPLOYEES MANAGER_ID  R
5  DEPARTMENTS    MANAGER_ID  R
```

2. Choose **Settings**, and then choose **Mapping Rules**.

3. Specify the Mapping rule for Data type conversions for the list of identified columns in Step1. You will need to specify 4 rules, one for each column as described below.
   [See the AWS documentation website for more details]

   Note that in a real-world scenario you would choose the data type based on your requirements.

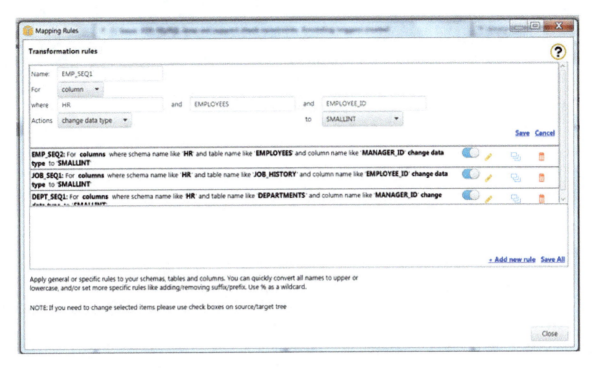

4. Choose **Yes** for "Would you like to save Mapping Rule settings?"

9. Right-click the HR schema, and then choose **Convert schema**.

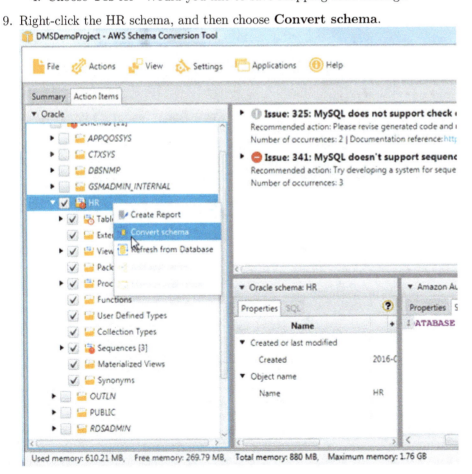

10. Choose **Yes** for the confirmation message. AWS SCT then converts your schema to the target database format.

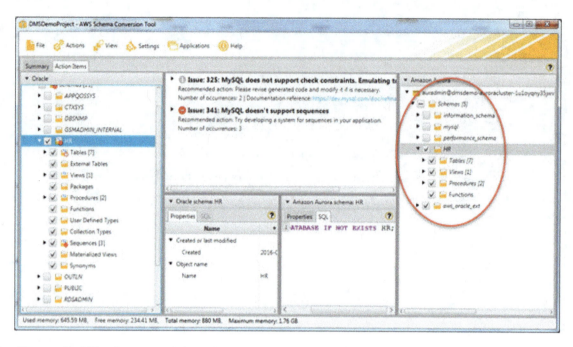

11. Choose the HR schema, and then choose **Apply to database** to apply the schema scripts to the target Aurora MySQL instance, as shown following.

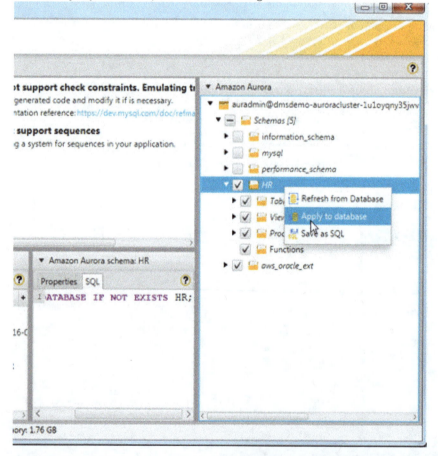

12. Choose the HR schema, and then choose **Refresh from Database** to refresh from the target database, as shown following.

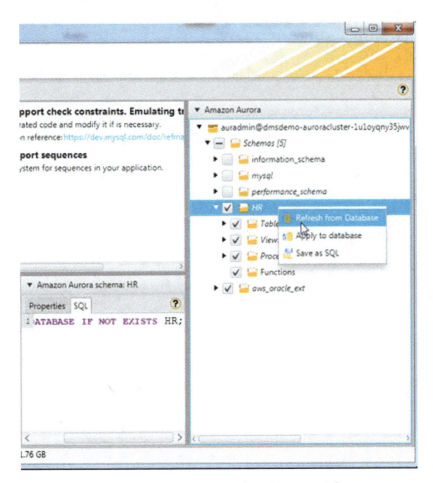

The database schema has now been converted and imported from source to target.

Step 6: Validate the Schema Conversion

To validate the schema conversion, you compare the objects found in the Oracle and Amazon Redshift databases using SQL Workbench/J.

To validate the schema conversion using SQL Workbench/J

1. In SQL Workbench/J, choose **File**, then choose **Connect window**. Choose the **RedshiftConnection** you created in an earlier step. Choose **OK**.

2. Run the following script to verify the number of object types and count in SH schema in the target Amazon Redshift database. These values should match the number of objects in the source Oracle database.

```
1 SELECT 'TABLE' AS OBJECT_TYPE,
2        TABLE_NAME AS OBJECT_NAME,
3        TABLE_SCHEMA AS OBJECT_SCHEMA
4 FROM information_schema.TABLES
5 WHERE TABLE_TYPE = 'BASE TABLE'
6 AND   OBJECT_SCHEMA = 'sh';
```

The output from this query should be similar to the following.

```
1 object_type | object_name | object_schema
2 ------------+-------------+---------------
3 TABLE       | channels    | sh
4 TABLE       | customers   | sh
5 TABLE       | products    | sh
6 TABLE       | promotions  | sh
7 TABLE       | sales       | sh
```

3. Verify the sort and distributions keys that are created in the Amazon Redshift cluster by using the following query.

```
1 set search_path to '$user', 'public', 'sh';
2
3 SELECT tablename,
4        "column",
5        TYPE,
6        encoding,
7        distkey,
8        sortkey,
9        "notnull"
10 FROM pg_table_def
11 WHERE (distkey = TRUE OR sortkey <> 0);
```

The results of the query reflect the distribution key (`distkey`) and sort key (`sortkey`) choices made by using AWS SCT key management.

tablename	column	type	encoding	distkey	sortkey	notnull
channels	channel_id	numeric(38,18)	none	true	1	true
customers	cust_id	numeric(38,18)	none	false	4	true
customers	cust_gender	character(2)	none	false	1	true

#	table	column	type				
6	customers	cust_year_of_birth	smallint	none	false		
					3	true	
7	customers	cust_marital_status	character varying(40)	none	false		
					2	false	
8	products	prod_id	integer	none	true		
					4	true	
9	products	prod_subcategory	character varying(100)	none	false		
					3	true	
10	products	prod_category	character varying(100)	none	false		
					2	true	
11	products	prod_status	character varying(40)	none	false		
					1	true	
12	promotions	promo_id	integer	none	true		
					1	true	
13	sales	prod_id	numeric(38,18)	none	false		
					4	true	
14	sales	cust_id	numeric(38,18)	none	false		
					3	true	
15	sales	time_id	timestamp without time zone	none	true		
					1	true	
16	sales	channel_id	numeric(38,18)	none	false		
					2	true	
17	sales	promo_id	numeric(38,18)	none	false		
					5	true	

Step 7: Create a AWS DMS Replication Instance

After we validate the schema structure between source and target databases, as described preceding, we proceed to the core part of this walkthrough, which is the data migration. The following illustration shows a high-level view of the migration process.

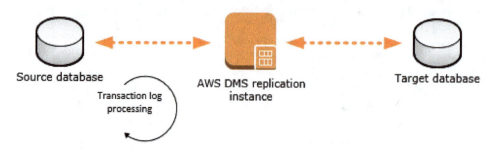

A DMS replication instance performs the actual data migration between source and target. The replication instance also caches the transaction logs during the migration. How much CPU and memory capacity a replication instance has influences the overall time required for the migration.

To create an AWS DMS replication instance

1. Sign in to the AWS Management Console, and select AWS DMS at https://console.aws.amazon.com/dms/ and choose **Create Migration**. If you are signed in as an AWS Identity and Access Management (IAM) user, you must have the appropriate permissions to access AWS DMS. For more information on the permissions required, see IAM Permissions Needed to Use AWS DMS.

2. Choose **Next** to start a database migration from the console's Welcome page.

3. On the **Create replication instance** page, specify your replication instance information as shown following.
   [See the AWS documentation website for more details]

4. For the **Advanced** section, leave the default settings as they are, and choose **Next**.

Step 8: Create AWS DMS Source and Target Endpoints

While your replication instance is being created, you can specify the source and target database endpoints using the AWS Management Console. However, you can only test connectivity after the replication instance has been created, because the replication instance is used in the connection.

To specify source or target database endpoints using the AWS console

1. Specify your connection information for the source Oracle database and the target Amazon Redshift database. The following table describes the source settings.
   [See the AWS documentation website for more details]

   The following table describes the target settings.
   [See the AWS documentation website for more details]

   The completed page should look like the following.

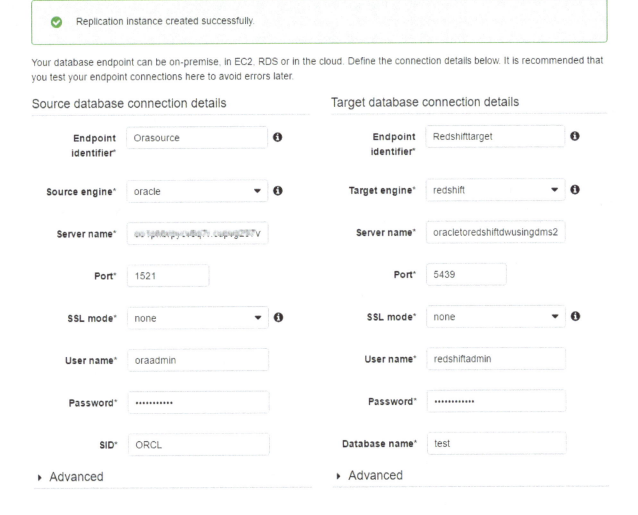

2. Wait for the status to say **Replication instance created successfully.**.

3. To test the source and target connections, choose **Run Test** for the source and target connections.

4. Choose **Next**.

Step 9: Create and Run Your AWS DMS Migration Task

Using an AWS DMS task, you can specify what schema to migrate and the type of migration. You can migrate existing data, migrate existing data and replicate ongoing changes, or replicate data changes only. This walkthrough migrates existing data only.

To create a migration task

1. On the **Create Task** page, specify the task options. The following table describes the settings. [See the AWS documentation website for more details]

   The page should look like the following.

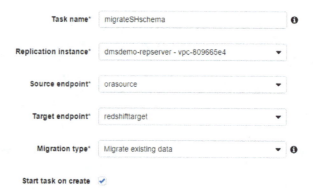

2. On the **Task Settings** section, specify the settings as shown in the following table. [See the AWS documentation website for more details]

   The section should look like the following.

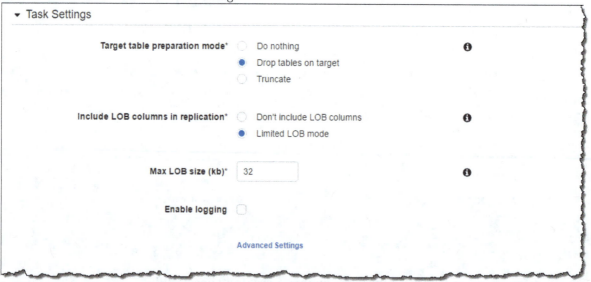

3. In the **Selection rules** section, specify the settings as shown in the following table. [See the AWS documentation website for more details]

   The section should look like the following:

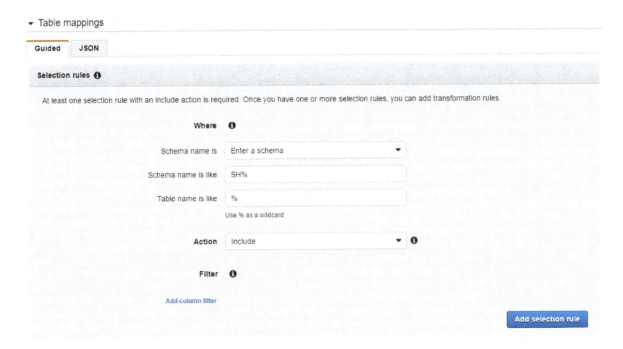

4. Choose **Add selection rule**.

5. Choose **Create task**.

5. Choose **Create task**. The task begins immediately. The **Tasks** section shows you the status of the migration task.

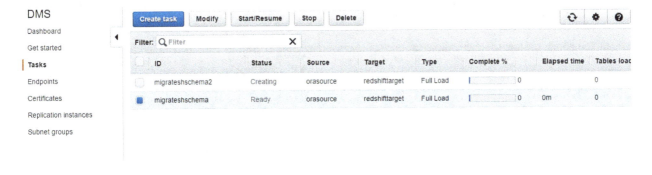

Step 10: Verify That Your Data Migration Completed Successfully

When the migration task completes, you can compare your task results with the expected results.

To compare your migration task results with the expected results

1. On the navigation pane, choose **Tasks**.

2. Choose your migration task (**migrateSHschema**).

3. Choose the **Table statistics** tab, shown following.

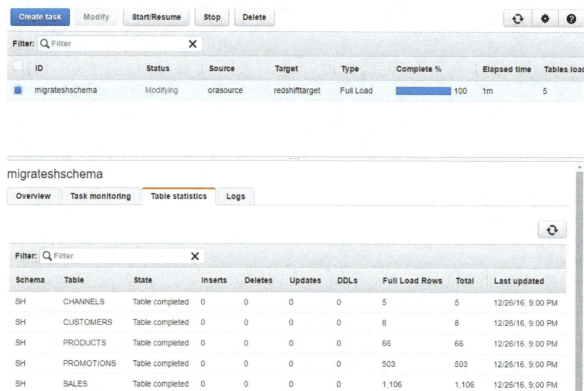

4. Connect to the Amazon Redshift instance by using SQL Workbench/J, and then check whether the database tables were successfully migrated from Oracle to Amazon Redshift by running the SQL script shown following.

```
1 select "table", tbl_rows
2 from svv_table_info
3 where
4 SCHEMA = 'sh'
5 order by 1;
```

Your results should look similar to the following.

```
1 table       | tbl_rows
2 ------------+----------
3 channels    |        5
4 customers   |        8
5 products    |       66
6 promotions  |      503
7 sales       |     1106
```

5. To verify whether the output for tables and number of rows from the preceding query matches what is expected for RDS Oracle, compare your results with those in previous steps.

6. Run the following query to check the relationship in tables; this query checks the departments with employees greater than 10.

```
1 Select b.channel_desc,count(*) from SH.SALES a,SH.CHANNELS b where a.channel_id=b.
    channel_id
2 group by b.channel_desc
3 order by 1;
```

The output from this query should be similar to the following.

```
1 channel_desc | count
2 -------------+------
3 Direct Sales |   355
4 Internet     |    26
5 Partners     |   172
```

7. Verify column compression encoding.

DMS uses an Amazon Redshift COPY operation to load data. By default, the COPY command applies automatic compression whenever loading to an empty target table. The sample data for this walkthrough is not large enough for automatic compression to be applied. When you migrate larger data sets, COPY will apply automatic compression.

For more details about automatic compression on Amazon Redshift tables, see Loading Tables with Automatic Compression.

To view compression encodings, run the following query.

```
1 SELECT *
2 FROM pg_table_def
3 WHERE schemaname = ''sh;
```

Now you have successfully completed a database migration from an Amazon RDS for Oracle DB instance to Amazon Redshift.

Step 11: Delete Walkthrough Resources

After you have completed this walkthrough, perform the following steps to avoid being charged further for AWS resources used in the walkthrough. It's necessary that you do the steps in order, because some resources cannot be deleted if they have a dependency upon another resource.

To delete AWS DMS resources

1. On the navigation pane, choose **Tasks**, choose your migration task (**migratehrschema**), and then choose **Delete**.

2. On the navigation pane, choose **Endpoints**, choose the Oracle source endpoint (**orasource**), and then choose **Delete**.

3. Choose the Amazon Redshift target endpoint (**redshifttarget**), and then choose **Delete**.

4. On the navigation pane, choose **Replication instances**, choose the replication instance (**DMSdemo-repserver**), and then choose **Delete**.

Next, you must delete your AWS CloudFormation stack, **DMSdemo**.

To delete your AWS CloudFormation stack

1. Sign in to the AWS Management Console and open the AWS CloudFormation console at https://console.aws.amazon.com/cloudformation.

   If you are signed in as an IAM user, you must have the appropriate permissions to access AWS CloudFormation.

2. Choose your CloudFormation stack, **OracletoRedshiftDWusingDMS**.

3. For **Actions**, choose **Delete stack**.

The status of the stack changes to DELETE_IN_PROGRESS while AWS CloudFormation cleans up the resources associated with the **OracletoRedshiftDWusingDMS** stack. When AWS CloudFormation is finished cleaning up resources, it removes the stack from the list.

Next Steps

You can explore several other features of AWS DMS that were not included in this walkthrough, including the following:

- The AWS DMS change data capture (CDC) feature, for ongoing replication of data.
- Transformation actions that let you specify and apply transformations to the selected schema or table as part of the migration process.

  For more information, see the AWS DMS documentation.

AWS CloudFormation Template, SQL Scripts, and Other Resources

You can find the AWS CloudFormation template, SQL scripts, and other resources used in this walkthrough on the AWS site as listed following:

- Oracle schema SQL script

- AWS CloudFormation template

- SQL validation script, in spreadsheet format

- SQL validation script, in text format

- Architecture diagram, in .jpg format or Architecture diagram, in .vsd format

- MySQL JDBC driver, in .jar file format

- Oracle Database 12.1.0.2 JDBC driver, in .jar file format

References

The following documentation and sample schemas can be useful as references for this walkthrough:

- AWS DMS documentation
- AWS SCT documentation
- Amazon Redshift documentation
- SQL statements to build the SH schema
- AWS CloudFormation template
- Oracle sample schemas

Migrating a SQL Server Database to Amazon Aurora MySQL

Using this walkthrough, you can learn how to migrate a Microsoft SQL Server database to an Amazon Aurora with MySQL compatibility database using the AWS Schema Conversion Tool (AWS SCT) and AWS Database Migration Service (AWS DMS). AWS DMS migrates your data from your SQL Server source into your Aurora MySQL target.

AWS DMS doesn't migrate your secondary indexes, sequences, default values, stored procedures, triggers, synonyms, views, and other schema objects that aren't specifically related to data migration. To migrate these objects to your Aurora MySQL target, use AWS SCT.

- Prerequisites
- Step-by-Step Migration
- Troubleshooting

Step 1: Install the SQL Drivers and AWS Schema Conversion Tool on Your Local Computer

Install the SQL drivers and the AWS Schema Conversion Tool (AWS SCT) on your local computer.

To install the SQL client software

1. Download the JDBC driver for your Oracle database release. For example, the Oracle Database 12.1.0.2 JDBC driver is (ojdbc7.jar).

2. Download the PostgreSQL driver (postgresql-42.1.4.jar).

3. Install AWS SCT and the required JDBC drivers.

   1. Download AWS SCT from Installing and Updating the AWS Schema Conversion Tool in the *AWS Schema Conversion Tool User Guide*.

   2. Launch AWS SCT.

   3. In AWS SCT, choose **Global Settings** from **Settings**.

   4. In **Global Settings**, choose **Driver**, and then choose **Browse** for **Oracle Driver Path**. Locate the JDBC Oracle driver and choose **OK**.

   5. Choose **Browse** for **PostgreSQL Driver Path**. Locate the JDBC PostgreSQL driver and choose **OK**.

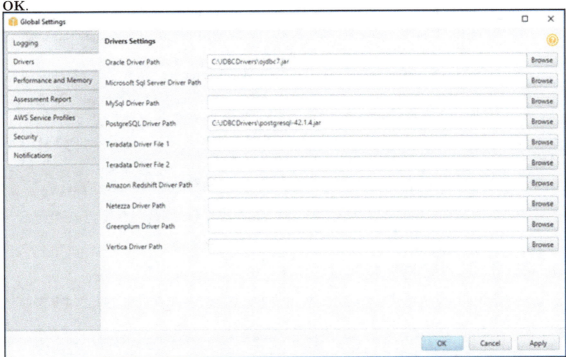

   6. Choose **OK** to close the dialog box.

Step 2: Configure Your Microsoft SQL Server Source Database

After installing the SQL drivers and AWS Schema Conversion Tool, you can configure your Microsoft SQL Server source database using one of several options, depending on how you plan to migrate your data.

To configure your SQL Server source database

- When configuring your source database, you can choose to migrate existing data only, migrate existing data and replicate ongoing changes, or migrate existing data and use change data capture (CDC) to replicate ongoing changes. For more information about these options, see Prerequisites.

    - Migrating existing data only

        No configuration steps are necessary for the SQL Server database. You can move on to Step 3: Configure Your Aurora MySQL Target Database. **Note**
        If the SQL Server database is an Amazon RDS database, replication is not supported, and you must use the option for migrating existing data only.

    - Migrating existing data and replicating ongoing changes **Note**
        Replication requires a primary key for all tables that are being replicated. If your tables don't have primary keys defined, consider using CDC instead.

        To configure MS-REPLICATION, complete the following steps:

        1. In Microsoft SQL Server Management Studio, open the context (right-click) menu for the **Replication** folder, and then choose **Configure Distribution**.

        2. In the **Distributor** step, choose *db_name* **will act as its own distributor**. SQL Server creates a distribution database and log.

            For more information, see the Microsoft documentation.

            When the configuration is complete, your server is enabled for replication. Either a distribution database is in place, or you have configured your server to use a remote distribution database.

- Migrating existing data and using change data capture (CDC) to replicate ongoing changes

    To configure MS-CDC, complete the following steps:

    1. Connect to SQL Server with a login that has SYSADMIN role membership.

    2. For each database containing data that is being migrated, run the following command within the database context:

```
1 use [DBname]
2 EXEC sys.sp_cdc_enable_db
```

    3. For each table that you want to configure for ongoing migration, run the following command:

```
1
2 EXEC sys.sp_cdc_enable_table @source_schema = N'schema_name', @source_name = N'
    table_name', @role_name = NULL;
```

        For more information, see the Microsoft documentation.

Note
If you are migrating databases that participate in an AlwaysOn Availability Group, it is best practice to use replication for migration. To use this option, publishing must be enabled, and a distribution database must be configured for each node of the AlwaysOn Availability Group. Additionally, ensure you are using the name of the availability group listener for the database rather than the name of the server currently hosting the availability group database for the target server name. These requirement apply to each instance of SQL Server in the cluster and must not be configured using the availability group listener. If your database isn't supported

for MS-REPLICATION or MS-CDC (for example, if you are running the Workgroup Edition of SQL Server), some changes can still be captured, such as `INSERT` and `DELETE` statements, but other DML statements such as `UPDATE` and `TRUNCATE TABLE` will not be captured. Therefore, a migration with continuing data replication is not recommended in this configuration, and a static one time migration (or repeated one time full migrations) should be considered instead.

For more information about using MS-REPLICATION and MS-CDC, see Configuring a Microsoft SQL Server Database as a Replication Source for AWS Database Migration Service.

Step 3: Configure Your Aurora MySQL Target Database

AWS DMS migrates the data from the SQL Server source into an Amazon Aurora MySQL target. In this step, you configure the Aurora MySQL target database.

1. Create the AWS DMS user to connect to your target database, and grant Superuser or the necessary individual privileges (or for Amazon RDS, use the master username).

   Alternatively, you can grant the privileges to an existing user.

```
1 CREATE USER 'aurora_dms_user' IDENTIFIED BY 'password';
2
3 GRANT ALTER, CREATE, DROP, INDEX, INSERT, UPDATE, DELETE,
4 SELECT ON target_database.* TO 'aurora_dms_user';
```

2. AWS DMS uses control tables on the target in the database `awsdms_control`. Use the following command to ensure that the user has the necessary access to the `awsdms_control` database:

```
1 GRANT ALL PRIVILEGES ON awsdms_control.* TO 'aurora_dms_user';
2 FLUSH PRIVILEGES;
```

Step 4: Use AWS SCT to Convert the SQL Server Schema to Aurora MySQL

Before you migrate data to Amazon Aurora MySQL, convert the Microsoft SQL Server schema to an Aurora MySQL schema using the AWS Schema Conversion Tool (AWS SCT).

To convert a SQL Server schema to an Aurora MySQL schema

1. In AWS SCT, choose **File**, **New Project**. Create a new project named **AWS Schema Conversion Tool SQL Server to Aurora MySQL**.

2. In the **New Project** dialog box, enter the following information, and then choose **OK**.
   [See the AWS documentation website for more details]

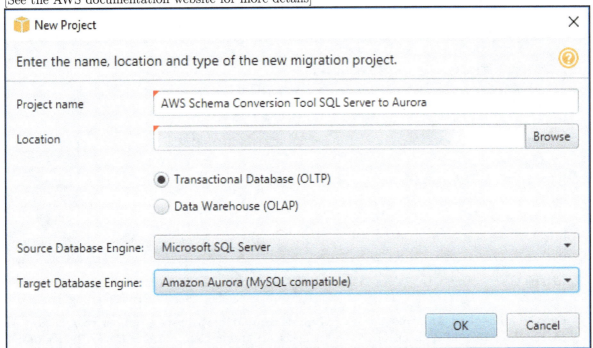

3. Choose **Connect to Microsoft SQL Server**. In the **Connect to Microsoft SQL Server** dialog box, enter the following information, and then choose **Test Connection**.
   [See the AWS documentation website for more details]

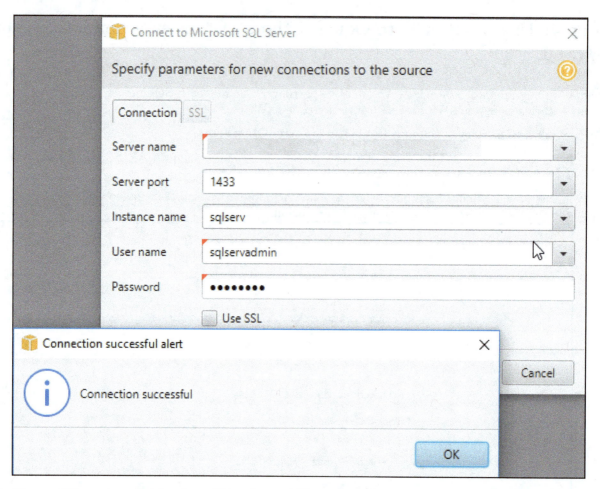

4. Choose **OK** to close the alert box. Then choose **OK** to close the dialog box and start the connection to the SQL Server DB instance. The database structure on the SQL Server DB instance is shown.

5. Choose **Connect to Amazon Aurora (MySQL compatible)**. In the **Connect to Amazon Aurora (MySQL compatible)** dialog box, enter the following information, and then choose **Test Connection**. [See the AWS documentation website for more details]

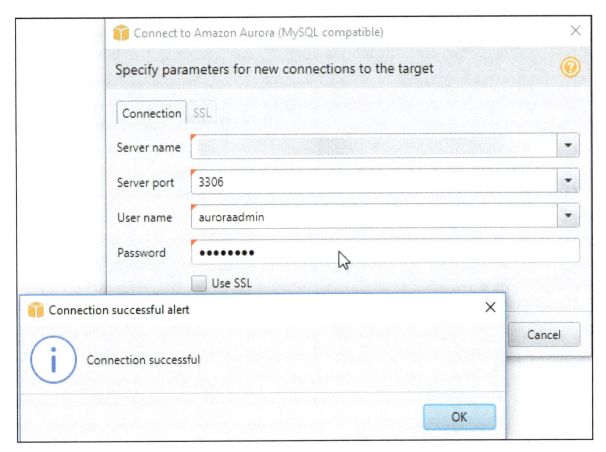

6. Choose **OK** to close the alert box. Then choose **OK** to close the dialog box and start the connection to the Aurora MySQL DB instance.

7. Open the context (right-click) menu for the schema to migrate, and then choose **Convert schema**.

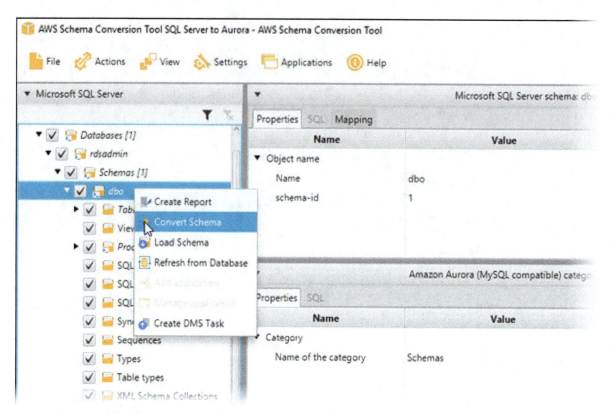

8. Choose **Yes** for the confirmation message. AWS SCT then converts your schemas to the target database format.

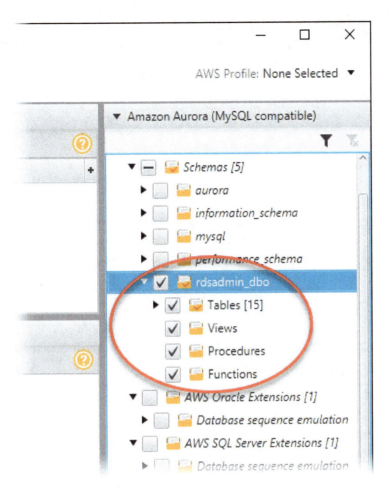

AWS SCT analyzes the schema and creates a database migration assessment report for the conversion to Aurora MySQL.

9. Choose **Assessment Report View** from **View** to check the report.

The report breaks down by each object type and by how much manual change is needed to convert it successfully.

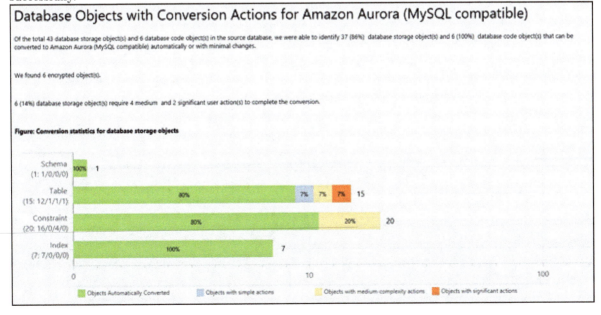

Generally, packages, procedures, and functions are more likely to have some issues to resolve because they contain the most custom PL/SQL code. AWS SCT also provides hints about how to fix these objects.

10. Choose the **Action Items** tab.

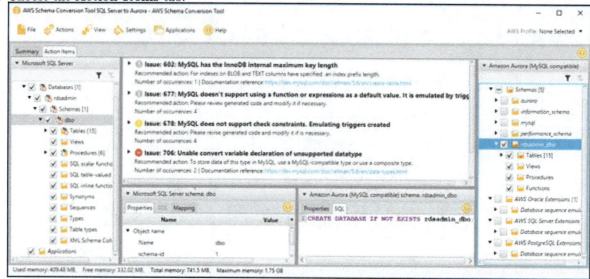

The **Action Items** tab shows each issue for each object that requires attention.

For each conversion issue, you can complete one of the following actions:

- Modify the objects on the source SQL Server database so that AWS SCT can convert the objects to the target Aurora MySQL database.

  1. Modify the objects on the source SQL Server database.

  2. Repeat the previous steps to convert the schema and check the assessment report.

  3. If necessary, repeat this process until there are no conversion issues.

  4. Choose **Main View** from **View**. Open the context (right-click) menu for the target Aurora MySQL schema, and choose **Apply to database** to apply the schema changes to the Aurora MySQL database, and confirm that you want to apply the schema changes.

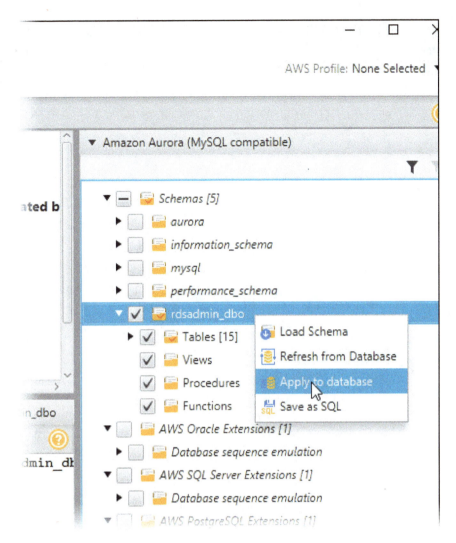

- Instead of modifying the source schema, modify scripts that AWS SCT generates before applying the scripts on the target Aurora MySQL database.

  1. Choose **Main View** from **View**. Open the context (right-click) menu for the target Aurora MySQL schema name, and choose **Save as SQL**. Next, choose a name and destination for the script.

  2. In the script, modify the objects to correct conversion issues.

     You can also exclude foreign key constraints, triggers, and secondary indexes from the script because they can cause problems during the migration. After the migration is complete, you can create these objects on the Aurora MySQL database.

  3. Run the script on the target Aurora MySQL database.

For more information, see Converting Database Schema to Amazon RDS by Using the AWS Schema Conversion Tool in the *AWS Schema Conversion Tool User Guide*.

11. (Optional) Use AWS SCT to create mapping rules.

    1. Under **Settings**, select **Mapping Rules**.

    2. Create additional mapping rules that are required based on the action items.

    3. Save the mapping rules.

4. Choose **Export script for DMS** to export a JSON format of all the transformations that the AWS DMS task will use. Choose **Save**.

Step 5: Create an AWS DMS Replication Instance

After validating the schema structure between source and target databases, continue with the core part of this walkthrough, which is the data migration. The following illustration shows a high-level view of the migration process.

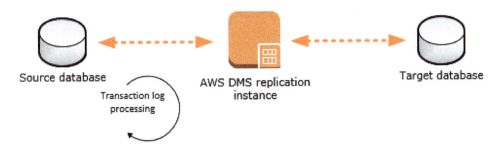

An AWS DMS replication instance performs the actual data migration between source and target. The replication instance also caches the transaction logs during the migration. How much CPU and memory capacity a replication instance has influences the overall time required for the migration.

To create an AWS DMS replication instance

1. Sign in to the AWS Management Console, and select AWS DMS at https://console.aws.amazon.com/dms/. Next, choose **Create Migration**. If you are signed in as an AWS Identity and Access Management (IAM) user, then you must have the appropriate permissions to access AWS DMS. For more information on the permissions required, see IAM Permissions Needed to Use AWS DMS.

2. Choose **Next** to start a database migration from the console's Welcome page.

3. On the **Create replication instance** page, specify your replication instance information.
   [See the AWS documentation website for more details]

4. For the **Advanced** section, specify the following information.
   [See the AWS documentation website for more details]

   For information about the KMS master key, see Setting an Encryption Key and Specifying KMS Permissions.

5. Click **Next**.

Step 6: Create AWS DMS Source and Target Endpoints

While your replication instance is being created, you can specify the source and target database endpoints using the AWS Management Console. However, you can only test connectivity after the replication instance has been created, because the replication instance is used in the connection.

To specify source and target database endpoints using the console

1. Specify your connection information for the source Oracle database and the target PostgreSQL database. The following table describes the source settings.
   [See the AWS documentation website for more details]

   The following table describes the advanced source settings.
   [See the AWS documentation website for more details]

   For information about extra connection attributes, see Using Extra Connection Attributes with AWS Database Migration Service.

   The following table describes the target settings.
   [See the AWS documentation website for more details]

   The following is an example of the completed page.

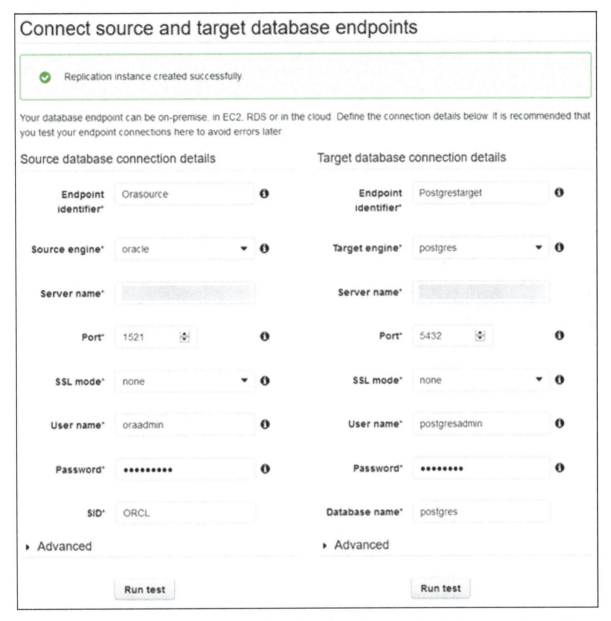

Connect source and target database endpoints

✓ Replication instance created successfully.

Your database endpoint can be on-premise, in EC2, RDS or in the cloud. Define the connection details below. It is recommended that you test your endpoint connections here to avoid errors later.

Source database connection details

Endpoint identifier*	Orasource
Source engine*	oracle ▼
Server name*	
Port*	1521
SSL mode*	none ▼
User name*	oraadmin
Password*	•••••••••
SID*	ORCL

▸ Advanced

Run test

Target database connection details

Endpoint identifier*	Postgrestarget
Target engine*	postgres ▼
Server name*	
Port*	5432
SSL mode*	none ▼
User name*	postgresadmin
Password*	••••••••
Database name*	postgres

▸ Advanced

Run test

2. After the endpoints and replication instance have been created, test each endpoint connection by choosing **Run test** for the source and target endpoints.

3. Drop foreign key constraints and triggers on the target database.

    During the full load process, AWS DMS does not load tables in any particular order, so it may load the child table data before parent table data. As a result, foreign key constraints might be violated if they are enabled. Also, if triggers are present on the target database, then it may change data loaded by AWS DMS in unexpected ways.

4. If you do not have one, then generate a script that enables the foreign key constraints and triggers.

    Later, when you want to add them to your migrated database, you can just run this script.

5. (Optional) Drop secondary indexes on the target database.

    Secondary indexes (as with all indexes) can slow down the full load of data into tables since they need to be maintained and updated during the loading process. Dropping them can improve the performance of your full load process. If you drop the indexes, then you will need to add them back later after the full load is complete.

6. Choose **Next**.

Step 7: Create and Run Your AWS DMS Migration Task

Using an AWS DMS task, you can specify which schema to migrate and the type of migration. You can migrate existing data, migrate existing data and replicate ongoing changes, or replicate data changes only. This walkthrough migrates existing data and replicates ongoing changes.

To create a migration task

1. On the **Create Task** page, specify the task options. The following table describes the settings.
   [See the AWS documentation website for more details]

   The page should look like the following:

   ## Create task

   A task can contain one or more table mappings which define what data is moved from the source to the target. If a table does not exist on the target, it can be created automatically.

Task name*	MigrateSchematoPostgres ❶
Task description*	Migrate a schema from Oracle to PostgreSQL ❶
Source endpoint	orasource
Target endpoint	postgrestarget
Replication instance	oracle2postgressql
Migration type*	Migrate existing data and replicate ongoing changes ▼ ❶

   Your source database is Oracle. Replicating ongoing changes requires supplemental logging to be turned on.

   Please ensure your archive logs are retained on the server for a sufficient amount of time. (24 hours is usually enough.) To set your archivelog retention on RDS databases you can use the following command exec rdsadmin.rdsadmin_util.set_configuration('archivelog retention hours', 24).

   Start task on create ✓

2. Under **Task Settings**, choose **Do nothing** or **Truncate** for **Target table preparation mode**, because you have already created the tables using the AWS Schema Conversion Tool.

   If the Oracle database has LOBs, then for **Include LOB columns in replication**, select **Full LOB mode** if you want to replicate the entire LOB for all tables. Select **Limited LOB mode** if you want to replicate the LOBs only up to a certain size. You specify the size of the LOB to migrate in **Max LOB size (kb)**.

   It is best to select **Enable logging**. If you enable logging, then you can see any errors or warnings that the task encounters, and you can troubleshoot those issues.

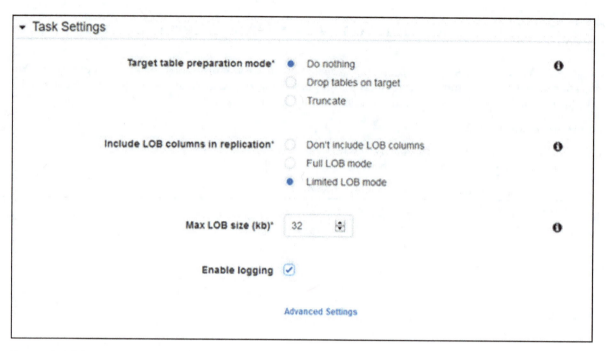

3. Leave the Advanced settings at their default values.

4. Choose **Table mappings**, and select the **JSON** tab. Next, select **Enable JSON editing**, and enter the table mappings you saved in the last step in Step 4: Use the AWS Schema Conversion Tool (AWS SCT) to Convert the Oracle Schema to PostgreSQL.

   The following is an example of mappings that convert schema names and table names to lowercase.

```
1
2  {
3    "rules": [
4      {
5        "rule-type": "transformation",
6        "rule-id": "100000",
7        "rule-name": "Default Lowercase Table Rule",
8        "rule-action": "convert-lowercase",
9        "rule-target": "table",
10       "object-locator": {
11         "schema-name": "%",
12         "table-name": "%"
13       }
14     },
15     {
16       "rule-type": "transformation",
17       "rule-id": "100001",
18       "rule-name": "Default Lowercase Schema Rule",
19       "rule-action": "convert-lowercase",
20       "rule-target": "schema",
21       "object-locator": {
22         "schema-name": "%"
23       }
24     }
25   ]
26 }
```

5. Choose **Create task**. The task will begin immediately.

The Tasks section shows you the status of the migration task.

You can monitor your task if you chose **Enable logging** when you set up your task. You can then view the CloudWatch metrics by doing the following:

To monitor a data migration task in progress

1. On the navigation pane, choose **Tasks**.

2. Choose your migration task.

3. Choose the **Task monitoring** tab, and monitor the task in progress on that tab.

   When the full load is complete and cached changes are applied, the task will stop on its own.

4. On the target PostgreSQL database, enable foreign key constraints and triggers using the script you saved previously.

5. On the target PostgreSQL database, re-create the secondary indexes if you removed them previously.

6. In the AWS DMS console, start the AWS DMS task by clicking **Start/Resume** for the task.

   The AWS DMS task keeps the target PostgreSQL database up-to-date with source database changes. AWS DMS will keep all of the tables in the task up-to-date until it is time to implement the application migration. The latency will be zero, or close to zero, when the target has caught up to the source.

Step 8: Cut Over to Aurora MySQL

Perform the following steps to move connections from your Microsoft SQL Server database to your Amazon Aurora MySQL database.

To cut over to Aurora MySQL

1. End all SQL Server database dependencies and activities, such as running scripts and client connections. Ensure that the SQL Server Agent service is stopped.

   The following query should return no results other than your connection:

   ```
   1 SELECT session_id, login_name from sys.dm_exec_sessions where session_id > 50;
   ```

2. Kill any remaining sessions (other than your own).

   ```
   1
   2 KILL session_id;
   ```

3. Shut down the SQL Server service.

4. Let the AWS DMS task apply the final changes from the SQL Server database on the Amazon Aurora MySQL database.

5. In the AWS DMS console, stop the AWS DMS task by choosing **Stop** for the task, and then confirming that you want to stop the task.

Migrating an Oracle Database to PostgreSQL

Using this walkthrough, you can learn how to migrate an Oracle database to a PostgreSQL database using AWS Database Migration Service (AWS DMS) and the AWS Schema Conversion Tool (AWS SCT).

AWS DMS migrates your data from your Oracle source into your PostgreSQL target. AWS DMS also captures data manipulation language (DML) and supported data definition language (DDL) changes that happen on your source database and applies these changes to your target database. This way, AWS DMS keeps your source and target databases in sync with each other. To facilitate the data migration, AWS SCT creates the migrated schemas on the target database, including the tables and primary key indexes on the target if necessary.

AWS DMS doesn't migrate your secondary indexes, sequences, default values, stored procedures, triggers, synonyms, views, and other schema objects not specifically related to data migration. To migrate these objects to your PostgreSQL target, use AWS SCT.

- Prerequisites
- Step-by-Step Migration
- Rolling Back the Migration
- Troubleshooting

Step 2: Configure Your Oracle Source Database

To use Oracle as a source for AWS Database Migration Service (AWS DMS), you must first ensure that ARCHIVELOG MODE is on to provide information to LogMiner. AWS DMS uses LogMiner to read information from the archive logs so that AWS DMS can capture changes.

For AWS DMS to read this information, make sure the archive logs are retained on the database server as long as AWS DMS requires them. If you configure your task to begin capturing changes immediately, then you should only need to retain archive logs for a little longer than the duration of the longest running transaction. Retaining archive logs for 24 hours is usually sufficient. If you configure your task to begin from a point in time in the past, then archive logs must be available from that time forward. For more specific instructions about enabling ARCHIVELOG MODE and ensuring log retention for your Oracle database, see the Oracle documentation.

To capture change data, AWS DMS requires supplemental logging to be enabled on your source database. Minimal supplemental logging must be enabled at the database level. AWS DMS also requires that identification key logging be enabled. This option causes the database to place all columns of a row's primary key in the redo log file whenever a row containing a primary key is updated. This result occurs even if no value in the primary key has changed. You can set this option at the database or table level.

To configure your Oracle source database

1. Create or configure a database account to be used by AWS DMS. We recommend that you use an account with the minimal privileges required by AWS DMS for your AWS DMS connection. AWS DMS requires the following privileges.

```
 1 CREATE SESSION
 2 SELECT ANY TRANSACTION
 3 SELECT on V_$ARCHIVED_LOG
 4 SELECT on V_$LOG
 5 SELECT on V_$LOGFILE
 6 SELECT on V_$DATABASE
 7 SELECT on V_$THREAD
 8 SELECT on V_$PARAMETER
 9 SELECT on V_$NLS_PARAMETERS
10 SELECT on V_$TIMEZONE_NAMES
11 SELECT on V_$TRANSACTION
12 SELECT on ALL_INDEXES
13 SELECT on ALL_OBJECTS
14 SELECT on ALL_TABLES
15 SELECT on ALL_USERS
16 SELECT on ALL_CATALOG
17 SELECT on ALL_CONSTRAINTS
18 SELECT on ALL_CONS_COLUMNS
19 SELECT on ALL_TAB_COLS
20 SELECT on ALL_IND_COLUMNS
21 SELECT on ALL_LOG_GROUPS
22 SELECT on SYS.DBA_REGISTRY
23 SELECT on SYS.OBJ$
24 SELECT on DBA_TABLESPACES
25 SELECT on ALL_TAB_PARTITIONS
26 SELECT on ALL_ENCRYPTED_COLUMNS
27 * SELECT on all tables migrated
```

If you want to capture and apply changes (CDC), then you also need the following privileges.

```
 1 EXECUTE on DBMS_LOGMNR
 2 SELECT on V_$LOGMNR_LOGS
```

```
3 SELECT on V_$LOGMNR_CONTENTS
4 LOGMINING /* For Oracle 12c and higher. */
5 * ALTER for any table being replicated (if you want AWS DMS to add supplemental logging)
```

For Oracle versions before 11.2.0.3, you need the following privileges.

```
1 SELECT on DBA_OBJECTS /* versions before 11.2.0.3 */
2 SELECT on ALL_VIEWS (required if views are exposed)
```

2. If your Oracle database is an AWS RDS database, then connect to it as an administrative user, and run the following command to ensure that archive logs are retained on your RDS source for 24 hours:

```
1 exec rdsadmin.rdsadmin_util.set_configuration('archivelog retention hours',24);
```

If your Oracle source is an AWS RDS database, it will be placed in ARCHIVELOG MODE if, and only if, you enable backups.

3. Run the following command to enable supplemental logging at the database level, which AWS DMS requires:

- In Oracle SQL:

```
1 ALTER DATABASE ADD SUPPLEMENTAL LOG DATA;
```

- In RDS:

```
1 exec rdsadmin.rdsadmin_util.alter_supplemental_logging('ADD');
```

4. Use the following command to enable identification key supplemental logging at the database level. AWS DMS requires supplemental key logging at the database level. The exception is if you allow AWS DMS to automatically add supplemental logging as needed or enable key-level supplemental logging at the table level:

- In Oracle SQL:

```
1 ALTER DATABASE ADD SUPPLEMENTAL LOG DATA (PRIMARY KEY) COLUMNS;
```

- In RDS:

```
1 exec rdsadmin.rdsadmin_util.alter_supplemental_logging('ADD','PRIMARY KEY');
```

Your source database incurs a small bit of overhead when key level supplemental logging is enabled. Therefore, if you are migrating only a subset of your tables, then you might want to enable key level supplemental logging at the table level.

5. To enable key level supplemental logging at the table level, use the following command.

```
1 ALTER TABLE table_name ADD SUPPLEMENTAL LOG DATA (PRIMARY KEY) COLUMNS;
```

If a table does not have a primary key, then you have two options.

- You can add supplemental logging on all columns involved in the first unique index on the table (sorted by index name).
- You can add supplemental logging on all columns of the table.

To add supplemental logging on a subset of columns in a table, such as those involved in a unique index, run the following command.

```
1 ALTER TABLE table_name
2   ADD SUPPLEMENTAL LOG GROUP example_log_group (column_list) ALWAYS;
```

To add supplemental logging for all columns of a table, run the following command.

```
1 ALTER TABLE table_name ADD SUPPLEMENTAL LOG DATA (ALL) COLUMNS;
```

6. Create a user for AWS SCT.

```
1 CREATE USER oracle_sct_user IDENTIFIED BY password;
2
3 GRANT CONNECT TO oracle_sct_user;
4 GRANT SELECT_CATALOG_ROLE TO oracle_sct_user;
5 GRANT SELECT ANY DICTIONARY TO oracle_sct_user;
```

Step 3: Configure Your PostgreSQL Target Database

1. If the schemas you are migrating do not exist on the PostgreSQL database, then create the schemas.

2. Create the AWS DMS user to connect to your target database, and grant Superuser or the necessary individual privileges (or use the master username for RDS).

```
1 CREATE USER postgresql_dms_user WITH PASSWORD 'password';
2 ALTER USER postgresql_dms_user WITH SUPERUSER;
```

3. Create a user for AWS SCT.

```
1 CREATE USER postgresql_sct_user WITH PASSWORD 'password';
2
3 GRANT CONNECT ON DATABASE database_name TO postgresql_sct_user;
4 GRANT USAGE ON SCHEMA schema_name TO postgresql_sct_user;
5 GRANT SELECT ON ALL TABLES IN SCHEMA schema_name TO postgresql_sct_user;
6 GRANT ALL ON SEQUENCIES IN SCHEMA schema_name TO postgresql_sct_user;
```

Step 4: Use the AWS Schema Conversion Tool (AWS SCT) to Convert the Oracle Schema to PostgreSQL

Before you migrate data to PostgreSQL, you convert the Oracle schema to a PostgreSQL schema.

To convert an Oracle schema to a PostgreSQL schema using AWS SCT

1. Launch AWS SCT. In AWS SCT, choose **File**, then choose **New Project**. Create a new project called **AWS Schema Conversion Tool Oracle to PostgreSQL**. Enter the following information in the New Project window and then choose **OK**.
   [See the AWS documentation website for more details]

2. Choose **Connect to Oracle**. In the **Connect to Oracle** dialog box, enter the following information, and then choose **Test Connection**.
   [See the AWS documentation website for more details]

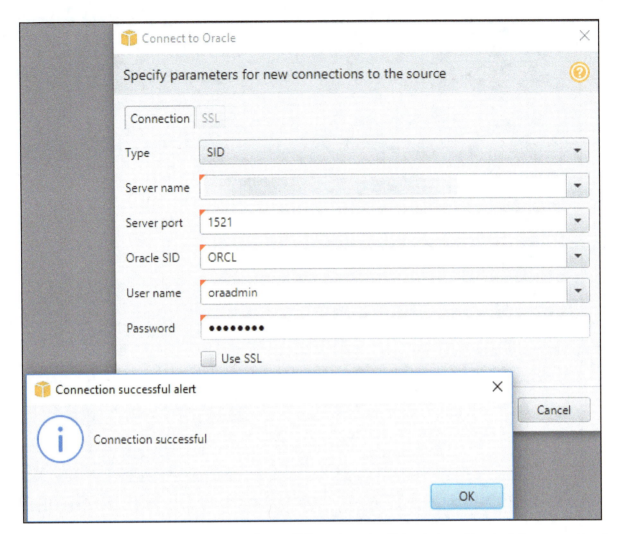

3. Choose **OK** to close the alert box, then choose **OK** to close the dialog box and to start the connection to the Oracle DB instance. The database structure on the Oracle DB instance is shown.

4. Choose **Connect to Amazon RDS for PostgreSQL**. In the **Connect to Amazon PostgreSQL** dialog box, enter the following information and then choose **Test Connection**.
   [See the AWS documentation website for more details]

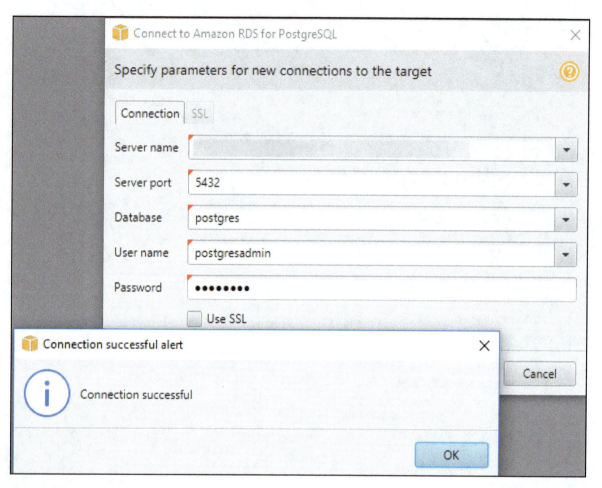

5. Choose **OK** to close the alert box, then choose **OK** to close the dialog box to start the connection to the PostgreSQL DB instance.

6. Open the context (right-click) menu for the schema to migrate, and then choose **Convert schema**.

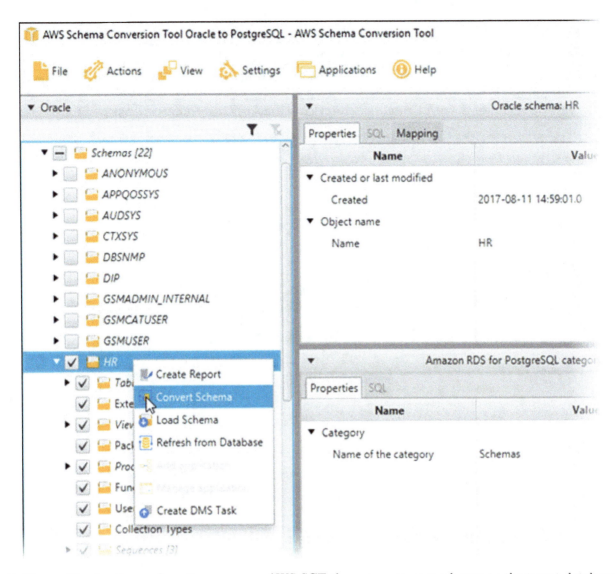

7. Choose **Yes** for the confirmation message. AWS SCT then converts your schemas to the target database format.

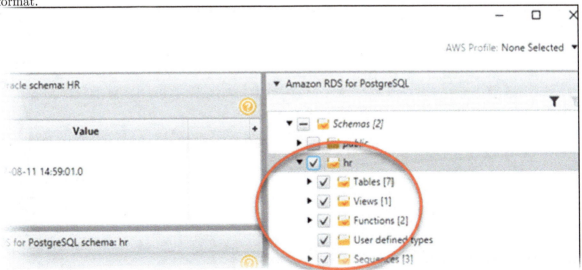

AWS SCT analyses the schema and creates a database migration assessment report for the conversion to

PostgreSQL.

8. Select **Assessment Report View** from **View** to check the report.

The report breaks down by each object type and by how much manual change is needed to successfully convert it.

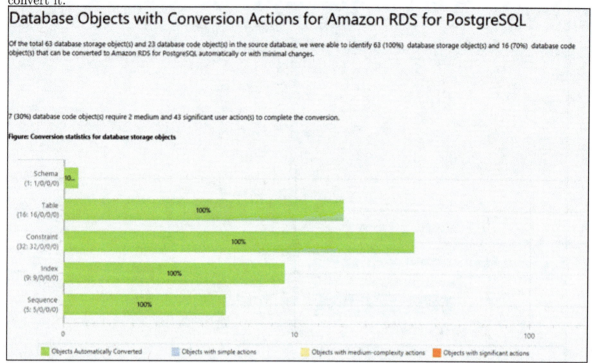

Generally packages, procedures, and functions are most likely to have some issues to resolve because they contain the most custom PL/SQL code. AWS SCT also provides hints about how to fix these objects.

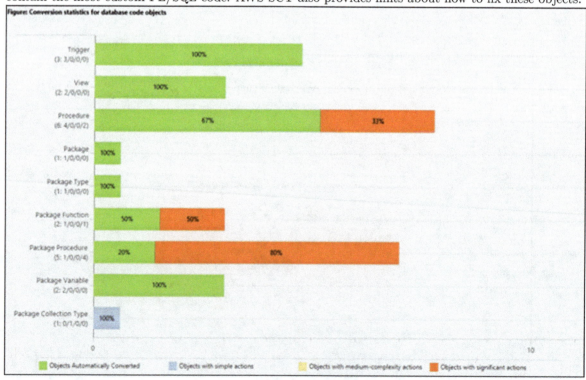

9. Choose the **Action Items** tab.

94

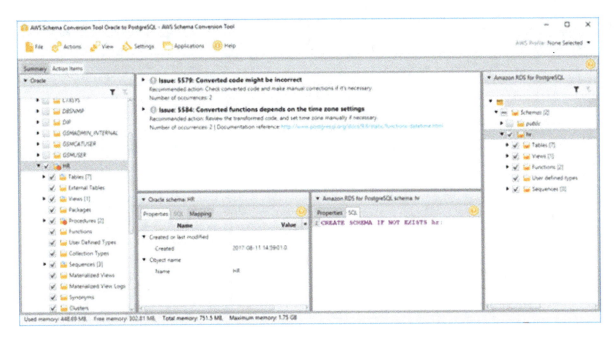

The **Action Items** tab shows each issue for each object that requires attention.

For each conversion issue, you can complete one of the following actions:

- Modify the objects on the source Oracle database so that AWS SCT can convert the objects to the target PostgreSQL database.

  1. Modify the objects on the source Oracle database.

  2. Repeat the previous steps to convert the schema and check the assessment report.

  3. If necessary, repeat this process until there are no conversion issues.

  4. Choose **Main View** from **View**, and open the context (right-click) menu for the target PostgreSQL schema, and choose **Apply to database** to apply the schema changes to the PostgreSQL database.

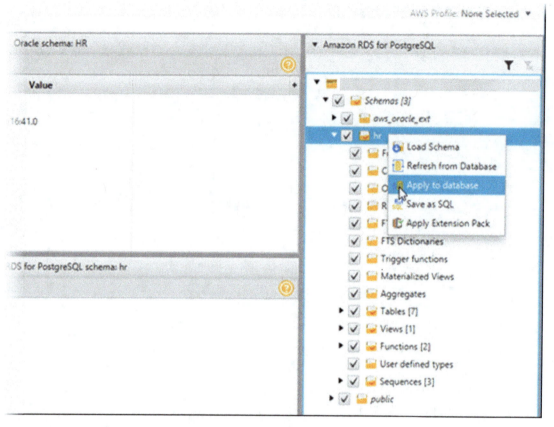

- Instead of modifying the source schema, modify scripts generated by AWS SCT before applying the scripts on the target PostgreSQL database.

    1. Open the context (right-click) menu for the target PostgreSQL schema name, and select **Save as SQL**. Next, choose a name and destination for the script.

    2. In the script, modify the objects to correct conversion issues.

    3. Run the script on the target PostgreSQL database.

For more information, see Converting Database Schema to Amazon RDS by Using the AWS Schema Conversion Tool in the *AWS Schema Conversion Tool User Guide*.

10. Use AWS SCT to create mapping rules.

    1. Under **Settings**, select **Mapping Rules**.

    2. In addition to the two default mapping rules that convert schema names and table names to lower case, create additional mapping rules that are required based on the action items.

    3. Save the mapping rules.

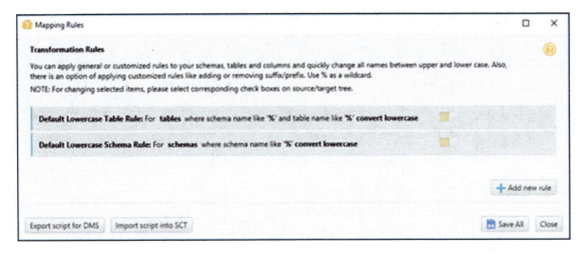

4. Click **Export script for DMS** to export a JSON format of all the transformations that the AWS DMS task will use to determine which object from the source corresponds to which object on the target. Click **Save**.

Step 8: Cut Over to PostgreSQL

Perform the following steps to move connections from your Oracle database to your PostgreSQL database.

To cut over to PostgreSQL

1. End all Oracle database dependencies and activities, such as running scripts and client connections.

   The following query should return no results:

   ```
   1 SELECT MACHINE, COUNT FROM V$SESSION GROUP BY MACHINE;
   ```

2. List any remaining sessions, and kill them.

   ```
   1 SELECT SID, SERIAL#, STATUS FROM V$SESSION;
   2
   3 ALTER SYSTEM KILL 'sid, serial_number' IMMEDIATE;
   ```

3. Shut down all listeners on the Oracle database.

4. Let the AWS DMS task apply the final changes from the Oracle database on the PostgreSQL database.

   ```
   1 ALTER SYSTEM CHECKPOINT;
   ```

5. In the AWS DMS console, stop the AWS DMS task by clicking **Stop** for the task, and confirm that you want to stop the task.

6. (Optional) Set up a rollback.

   You can optionally set up a rollback task, in case you run into a show stopping issue, by creating a task going in the opposite direction. Because all tables should be in sync between both databases, you only need to set up a CDC task. Therefore, you do not have to disable any foreign key constraints. Now that the source and target databases are reversed, you must follow the instructions in the following sections:

   - Using a PostgreSQL Database as a Source for AWS Database Migration Service
   - Using an Oracle Database as a Target for AWS Database Migration Service

   1. Disable triggers on the source Oracle database.

      ```
      1 SELECT 'ALTER TRIGGER' || owner || '.' || trigger_name || 'DISABLE;'
      2   FROM DBA_TRIGGERS WHERE OWNER = 'schema_name';
      ```

      You do not have to disable the foreign key constraints. During the CDC process, foreign key constraints are updated in the same order as they are updated by application users.

   2. Create a new CDC-only AWS DMS task with the endpoints reversed (source PostgreSQL endpoint and target Oracle endpoint database). See Step 7: Create and Run Your AWS DMS Migration Task.

      For the rollback task, set **Migration type** to **Replicate data changes only** and **Target table preparation mode** to **Do nothing**.

   3. Start the AWS DMS task to enable you to push changes back to the original source Oracle database from the new PostgreSQL database if rollback is necessary.

7. Connect to the PostgreSQL database, and enable triggers.

   ```
   1 ALTER TABLE table_name ENABLE TRIGGER ALL;
   ```

8. If you set up a rollback, then complete the rollback setup.

   1. Start the application services on new target PostgreSQL database (including scripts , client software, and so on).

   2. Add Cloudwatch monitoring on your new PostgreSQL database. See Monitoring Amazon RDS.

Rolling Back the Migration

If there are major issues with the migration that cannot be resolved in a timely manner, you can roll back the migration. These steps assume that you have already prepared for the rollback as described in Step 8: Cut Over to PostgreSQL.

To roll back the migration

1. Stop all application services on the target PostgreSQL database.

2. Let the AWS DMS task replicate remaining changes back to the source Oracle database.

3. Stop the PostgreSQL to Oracle AWS DMS task.

4. Start all applications back on the source Oracle database.

Migrating an Amazon RDS for Oracle Database to Amazon Redshift

This walkthrough gets you started with heterogeneous database migration from Amazon RDS for Oracle to Amazon Redshift using AWS Database Migration Service (AWS DMS) and the AWS Schema Conversion Tool (AWS SCT). This introductory exercise doesn't cover all scenarios but provides you with a good understanding of the steps involved in such a migration.

It is important to understand that AWS DMS and AWS SCT are two different tools and serve different needs. They don't interact with each other in the migration process. At a high level, the steps involved in this migration are the following:

1. Using the AWS SCT to do the following:

- Run the conversion report for Oracle to Amazon Redshift to identify the issues, limitations, and actions required for the schema conversion.

- Generate the schema scripts and apply them on the target before performing the data load by using AWS DMS. AWS SCT performs the necessary code conversion for objects like procedures and views.

1. Identify and implement solutions to the issues reported by AWS SCT.

2. Disable foreign keys or any other constraints that might impact the AWS DMS data load.

3. AWS DMS loads the data from source to target using the Full Load approach. Although AWS DMS is capable of creating objects in the target as part of the load, it follows a minimalistic approach to efficiently migrate the data so that it doesn't copy the entire schema structure from source to target.

4. Perform postmigration activities such as creating additional indexes, enabling foreign keys, and making the necessary changes in the application to point to the new database.

This walkthrough uses a custom AWS CloudFormation template to create RDS DB instances for Oracle and Amazon Redshift. It then uses a SQL command script to install a sample schema and data onto the RDS Oracle DB instance that you then migrate to Amazon Redshift.

This walkthrough takes approximately two hours to complete. Be sure to follow the instructions to delete resources at the end of this walkthrough to avoid additional charges.

- Prerequisites
- Migration Architecture
- Step-by-Step Migration
- Next Steps
- References

Step 4: Test the Connectivity to the Amazon Redshift Database

Next, test your connection to your Amazon Redshift database.

To test the connection to your Amazon Redshift database using SQL Workbench/J

1. In SQL Workbench/J, choose **File**, then choose **Connect window**. Choose the **Create a new connection profile** icon. Connect to the Amazon Redshift database in SQL Workbench/J by using the information shown following.
   [See the AWS documentation website for more details]

2. Test the connection by choosing **Test**. Choose **OK** to close the dialog box, then choose **OK** to create the connection profile.

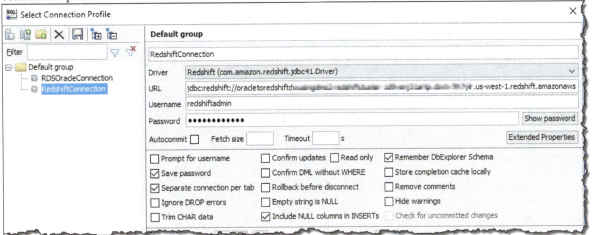

Note

If your connection is unsuccessful, ensure that the IP address you assigned when creating the CloudFormation template is the one you are attempting to connect from. This issue is the most common one when trying to connect to an instance.

3. Verify your connectivity to the Amazon Redshift DB instance by running a sample SQL command, such as `select current_date;`.

Step 5: Use AWS SCT to Convert the Oracle Schema to Amazon Redshift

Before you migrate data to Amazon Redshift, you convert the Oracle schema to an Amazon Redshift schema as described following.

To convert an Oracle schema to an Amazon Redshift schema using AWS SCT

1. Launch AWS SCT. In AWS SCT, choose **File**, then choose **New Project**. Create a new project called **DWSchemaMigrationDemoProject**. Enter the following information in the New Project window, and then choose **OK**.
   [See the AWS documentation website for more details]

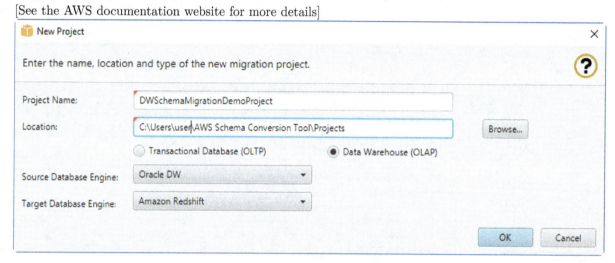

2. Choose **Connect to Oracle**. In the **Connect to Oracle** dialog box, enter the following information, and then choose **Test Connection**.
   [See the AWS documentation website for more details]

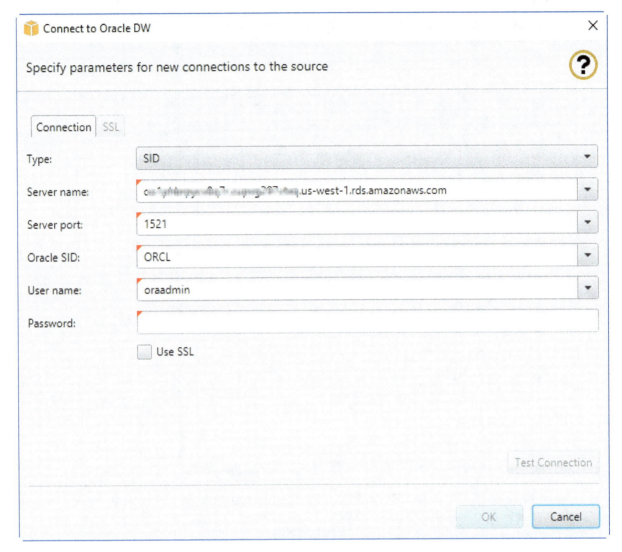

3. Choose **OK** to close the alert box, then choose OK to close the dialog box and to start the connection to the Oracle DB instance. The database structure on the Oracle DB instance is shown following. Select only the SH schema. **Note**

If the SH schema does not appear in the list, choose **Actions**, then choose **Refresh from Database**.

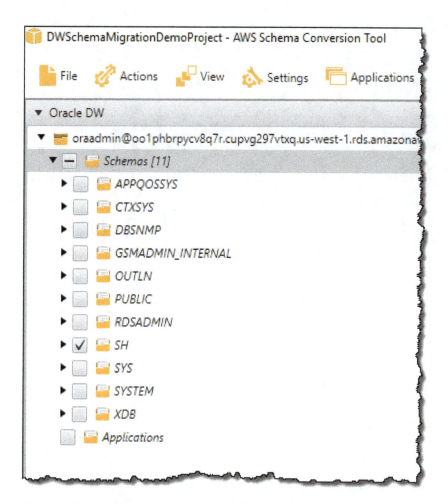

4. Choose **Connect to Amazon Redshift**. In the **Connect to Amazon Redshift** dialog box, enter the following information and then choose **Test Connection**.
[See the AWS documentation website for more details]

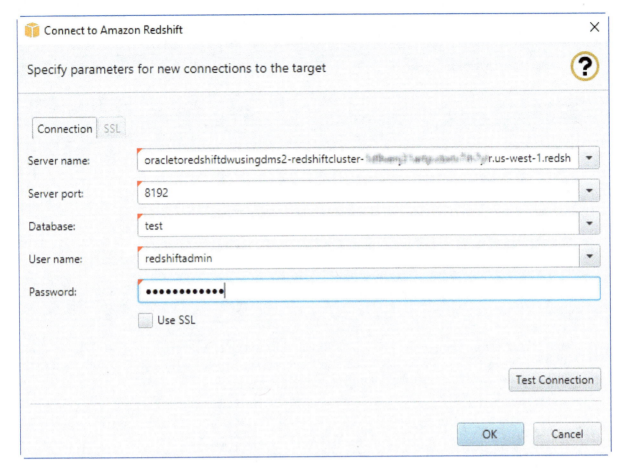

AWS SCT analyzes the SH schema and creates a database migration assessment report for the conversion to Amazon Redshift.

5. Choose **OK** to close the alert box, then choose **OK** to close the dialog box to start the connection to the Amazon Redshift DB instance.

6. In the **Oracle DW** view, open the context (right-click) menu for the **SH** schema and select **Create Report**.

7. Review the report summary. To save the report, choose either **Save to CSV** or **Save to PDF**.

The report discusses the type of objects that can be converted by using AWS SCT, along with potential migration issues and actions to resolve these issues. For this walkthrough, you should see something like the following.

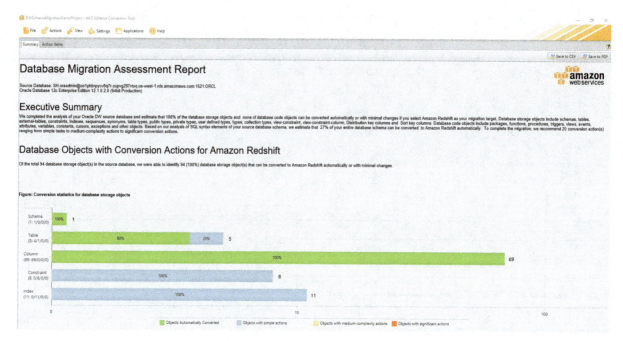

8. Choose the **Action Items** tab. The report discusses the type of objects that can be converted by using AWS SCT, along with potential migration issues and actions to resolve these issues. For this walkthrough, you should see something like the following.

9. Open the context (right-click) menu for the **SH** item in the **Schemas** list, and then choose **Collect Statistics**. AWS SCT analyzes the source data to recommend the best keys for the target Amazon Redshift database. For more information, see Collecting or Uploading Statistics for the AWS Schema Conversion Tool.

10. Open the context (right-click) menu for the **SH** schema, and then choose **Convert schema**.

11. Choose **Yes** for the confirmation message. AWS SCT then converts your schema to the target database format.

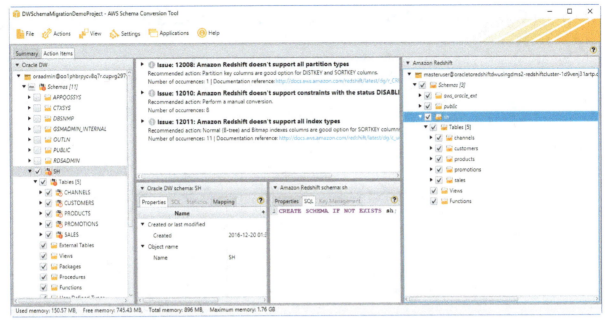

Note

The choice of the Amazon Redshift sort keys and distribution keys is critical for optimal performance. You can use key management in AWS SCT to customize the choice of keys. For this walkthrough, we use the defaults recommended by AWS SCT. For more information, see Optimizing Amazon Redshift by Using the AWS Schema Conversion Tool.

12. In the Amazon Redshift view, open the context (right-click) menu for the **SH** schema, and then choose **Apply to database** to apply the schema scripts to the target Amazon Redshift instance.

13. Open the context (right-click) menu for the **SH** schema, and then choose **Refresh from Database** to refresh from the target database.

The database schema has now been converted and imported from source to target.

Step 7: Create an AWS DMS Replication Instance

After we validate the schema structure between source and target databases, as described preceding, we proceed to the core part of this walkthrough, which is the data migration. The following illustration shows a high-level view of the migration process.

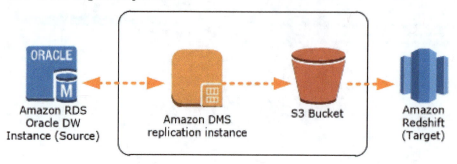

A DMS replication instance performs the actual data migration between source and target. The replication instance also caches the transaction logs during the migration. How much CPU and memory capacity a replication instance has influences the overall time required for the migration.

To create an AWS DMS replication instance

1. Sign in to the AWS Management Console, open the AWS DMS console at https://console.aws.amazon.com/dms/, and choose **Create Migration**. If you are signed in as an AWS Identity and Access Management (IAM) user, you must have the appropriate permissions to access AWS DMS. For more information on the permissions required, see IAM Permissions Needed to Use AWS DMS.

2. Choose **Create migration** to start a database migration.

3. On the **Welcome** page, choose **Next**.

4. On the **Create replication instance** page, specify your replication instance information as shown following.
[See the AWS documentation website for more details]

5. For the **Advanced** section, leave the default settings as they are, and choose **Next**.

Migrating MySQL-Compatible Databases to AWS

Amazon Web Services (AWS) has several services that allow you to run a MySQL-compatible database on AWS. Amazon Relational Database Service (Amazon RDS) supports MySQL-compatible databases including MySQL, MariaDB, and Amazon Aurora MySQL. AWS Elastic Cloud Computing Service (EC2) provides platforms for running MySQL-compatible databases.

Migrating From	Solution
An RDS MySQL DB instance	You can migrate data directly from an Amazon RDS MySQL DB snapshot to an Amazon Aurora MySQL DB cluster. For details, see Migrating Data from an Amazon RDS MySQL DB Instance to an Amazon Aurora MySQL DB Cluster.
A MySQL database external to Amazon RDS	If your database supports the InnoDB or MyISAM tablespaces, you have these options for migrating your data to an Amazon Aurora MySQL DB cluster: [See the AWS documentation website for more details] For details, see Migrating MySQL to Amazon Aurora MySQL by Using mysqldump.
A database that is not MySQL-compatible	You can also use AWS Database Migration Service (AWS DMS) to migrate data from a MySQL database. However, for very large databases, you can significantly reduce the amount of time that it takes to migrate your data by copying the source files for your database and restoring those files to an Amazon Aurora MySQL DB instance as described in Migrating Data from an External MySQL Database to an Amazon Aurora MySQL Using Amazon S3. For more information on AWS DMS, see What Is AWS Database Migration Service?

Migrating a MySQL-Compatible Database to Amazon Aurora MySQL

If your database supports the InnoDB or MyISAM tablespaces, you have these options for migrating your data to an Amazon Aurora MySQL DB cluster:

- You can create a dump of your data using the `mysqldump` utility, and then import that data into an existing Amazon Aurora MySQL DB cluster. For more information, see Migrating MySQL to Amazon Aurora MySQL by Using mysqldump.

- You can copy the source files from your database to an S3 bucket, and then restore an Amazon Aurora MySQL DB cluster from those files. This option can be considerably faster than migrating data using `mysqldump`. For more information, see Migrating Data from an External MySQL Database to an Amazon Aurora MySQL Using Amazon S3.

Migrating Data from an External MySQL Database to an Amazon Aurora MySQL Using Amazon S3

You can copy the source files from your source MySQL version 5.5 or 5.6 database to an S3 bucket, and then restore an Amazon Aurora MySQL DB cluster from those files.

This option can be considerably faster than migrating data using `mysqldump`, because using `mysqldump` replays all of the commands to recreate the schema and data from your source database in your new Amazon Aurora MySQL DB cluster. By copying your source MySQL data files, Amazon Aurora MySQL can immediately use those files as the data for DB cluster.

Note
Restoring an Amazon Aurora MySQL DB cluster from backup files in an S3 bucket is not supported for the Asia Pacific (Mumbai) region.

Amazon Aurora MySQL does not restore everything from your database. You should save the database schema and values for the following items from your source MySQL or MariaDB database and add them to your restored Amazon Aurora MySQL DB cluster after it has been created.

- User accounts
- Functions
- Stored procedures
- Time zone information. Time zone information is loaded from the local operating system of your Amazon Aurora MySQL DB cluster.

Prerequisites

Before you can copy your data to an S3 bucket and restore a DB cluster from those files, you must do the following:

- Install Percona XtraBackup on your local server.
- Permit Amazon Aurora MySQL to access your S3 bucket on your behalf.

Installing Percona XtraBackup

Amazon Aurora MySQL can restore a DB cluster from files that were created using Percona XtraBackup. You can install Percona XtraBackup from the Percona website at https://www.percona.com/doc/percona-xtrabackup/2.4/installation.

Required Permissions

To migrate your MySQL data to an Amazon Aurora MySQL DB cluster, several permissions are required:

- The user that is requesting that Amazon RDS create a new cluster from an S3 bucket must have permission to list the buckets for your AWS account. You grant the user this permission using an AWS Identity and Access Management (IAM) policy.

- Amazon RDS requires permission to act on your behalf to access the S3 bucket where you store the files used to create your Amazon Aurora MySQL DB cluster. You grant Amazon RDS the required permissions using an IAM service role.

- The user making the request must also have permission to list the IAM roles for your AWS account.

- If the user making the request will create the IAM service role, or will request that Amazon RDS create the IAM service role (by using the console), then the user must have permission to create an IAM role for your AWS account.

For example, the following IAM policy grants a user the minimum required permissions to use the console to both list IAM roles, create an IAM role, and list the S3 buckets for your account.

```
{
    "Version": "2012-10-17",
    "Statement": [
        {
            "Effect": "Allow",
            "Action": [
                "iam:ListRoles",
                "iam:CreateRole",
                "iam:CreatePolicy",
                "iam:AttachRolePolicy",
                "s3:ListBucket",
                "s3:ListObjects"
            ],
            "Resource": "*"
        }
    ]
}
```

Additionally, for a user to associate an IAM role with an S3 bucket, the IAM user must have the `iam:PassRole` permission for that IAM role. This permission allows an administrator to restrict which IAM roles a user can associate with S3 buckets.

For example, the following IAM policy allows a user to associate the role named `S3Access` with an S3 bucket.

```
{
    "Version":"2012-10-17",
    "Statement":[
        {
            "Sid":"AllowS3AccessRole",
            "Effect":"Allow",
            "Action":"iam:PassRole",
            "Resource":"arn:aws:iam::123456789012:role/S3Access"
        }
    ]
}
```

Creating the IAM Service Role

You can have the Amazon RDS Management Console create a role for you by choosing the **Create a New Role** option (shown later in this topic). If you select this option and specify a name for the new role, then Amazon RDS will create the IAM service role required for Amazon RDS to access your S3 bucket with the name that you supply.

As an alternative, you can manually create the role using the following procedure.

To create an IAM role for Amazon RDS to access S3

1. Sign in to the AWS Management Console and open the IAM console at https://console.aws.amazon.com/iam/.

2. In the left navigation pane, choose **Roles**.

3. Choose **Create New Role**, specify a value for **Role Name** for the new role, and then choose **Next Step**.

4. Under **AWS Service Roles**, find **Amazon RDS** and choose **Select**.

5. Do not select a policy to attach in the **Attach Policy** step. Instead, choose **Next Step**.

6. Review your role information, and then choose **Create Role**.

7. In the list of roles, choose the name of your newly created role. Choose the **Permissions** tab.

8. Choose **Inline Policies**. Because your new role has no policy attached, you will be prompted to create one. Click the link to create a new policy.

9. On the **Set Permissions** page, choose **Custom Policy** and then choose **Select**.

10. Type a **Policy Name** such as S3-bucket-policy. Add the following code for **Policy Document**, replacing with the name of the S3 bucket that you are allowing access to.

    As part of the policy document, you can also include a file name prefix. If you specify a prefix, then Amazon Aurora MySQL will create the DB cluster using the files in the S3 bucket that begin with the specified prefix. If you don't specify a prefix, then Amazon Aurora MySQL will create the DB cluster using all of the files in the S3 bucket.

    To specify a prefix, replace following with the prefix of your file names. Include the asterisk (*) after the prefix. If you don't want to specify a prefix, specify only an asterisk.

```
 1 {
 2     "Version": "2012-10-17",
 3     "Statement": [
 4         {
 5             "Effect": "Allow",
 6             "Action": [
 7                 "s3:ListBucket",
 8                 "s3:GetBucketLocation"
 9             ],
10             "Resource": [
11                 "arn:aws:s3:::<bucket name>"
12             ]
13         },
14         {
15             "Effect": "Allow",
16             "Action": [
17                 "s3:GetObject"
18             ],
19             "Resource": [
20                 "arn:aws:s3:::<bucket name>/<prefix>*"
```

```
21            ]
22          }
23      ]
24 }
```

11. Choose **Apply Policy**.

Step 1: Backing Up Files to be Restored as a DB Cluster

To create a backup of your MySQL database files that can be restored from S3 to create an Amazon Aurora MySQL DB cluster, use the Percona Xtrabackup utility (**innobackupex**) to back up your database.

For example, the following command creates a backup of a MySQL database and stores the files in the /s3-restore/backup folder.

```
1 innobackupex --user=myuser --password=<password> --no-timestamp /s3-restore/backup
```

If you want to compress your backup into a single file (which can be split, if needed), you can use the **--stream** option to save your backup in one of the following formats:

- Gzip (.gz)
- tar (.tar)
- Percona xbstream (.xbstream)

For example, the following command creates a backup of your MySQL database split into multiple Gzip files. The parameter values shown are for a small test database; for your scenario, you should determine the parameter values needed.

```
1 innobackupex --user=myuser --password=<password> --stream=tar \
2    /mydata/s3-restore/backup | split -d --bytes=512000 \
3    - /mydata/s3-restore/backup3/backup.tar.gz
```

For example, the following command creates a backup of your MySQL database split into multiple tar files.

```
1 innobackupex --user=myuser --password=<password> --stream=tar \
2    /mydata/s3-restore/backup | split -d --bytes=512000 \
3    - /mydata/s3-restore/backup3/backup.tar
```

For example, the following command creates a backup of your MySQL database split into multiple xbstream files.

```
1 innobackupex --stream=xbstream  \
2    /mydata/s3-restore/backup | split -d --bytes=512000 \
3    - /mydata/s3-restore/backup/backup.xbstream
```

S3 limits the size of a file uploaded to a bucket to 5 terabytes (TB). If the backup data for your database exceeds 5 TB, then you must use the **split** command to split the backup files into multiple files that are each less than 5 TB.

Amazon Aurora MySQL does not support partial backups created using Percona Xtrabackup. You cannot use the **--include**, **--tables-file**, or **--databases** options to create a partial backup when you backup the source files for your database.

For more information, see the The innobackupex Script.

Amazon Aurora MySQL consumes your backup files based on the file name. Be sure to name your backup files with the appropriate file extension based on the file format—for example, .**xbstream** for files stored using the Percona xbstream format.

113

Amazon Aurora MySQL consumes your backup files in alphabetical order as well as natural number order. Always use the `split` option when you issue the `innobackupex` command to ensure that your backup files are written and named in the proper order.

Step 2: Copying Files to an Amazon S3 Bucket

Once you have backed up your MySQL database using the Percona Xtrabackup utility, then you can copy your backup files to an S3 bucket.

For information on creating and uploading a file to an S3 bucket, see Getting Started with Amazon Simple Storage Service in the *Amazon S3 Getting Started Guide*.

Step 3: Restoring an Aurora MySQL DB Cluster from an S3 Bucket

You can restore your backup files from your Amazon S3 bucket to a create new Amazon Aurora MySQL DB cluster by using the Amazon RDS console.

To restore an Amazon Aurora MySQL DB cluster from files on an S3 bucket

1. Sign in to the AWS Management Console and open the Amazon RDS console at https://console.aws.amazon.com/rds/.

2. In the RDS Dashboard, choose **Restore Aurora MySQL DB Cluster from S3**.

3. In the **Specify Source Backup Details**, specify the following:
   [See the AWS documentation website for more details]

4. Choose **Next Step**.

5. On the **Specify DB Details** page, specify your DB cluster information. The following table shows settings for a DB instance.
   [See the AWS documentation website for more details]

   A typical **Specify DB Details** page looks like the following.

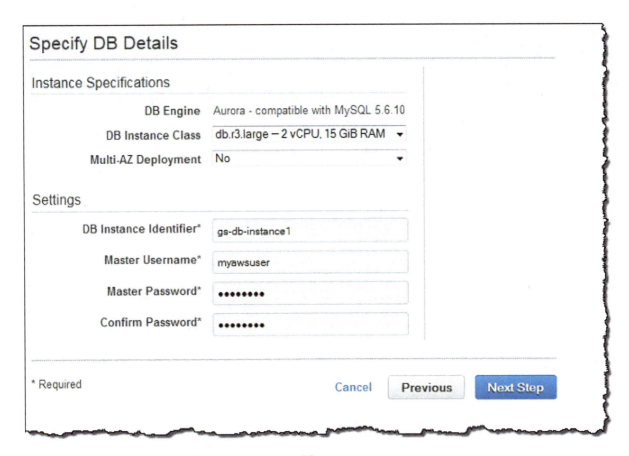

6. Confirm your master password, and then choose **Next**.

7. On the **Configure Advanced Settings** page, you can customize additional settings for your Aurora MySQL DB cluster. The following table shows the advanced settings for a DB cluster.
[See the AWS documentation website for more details]

A typical **Configure Advanced Settings** page looks like the following.

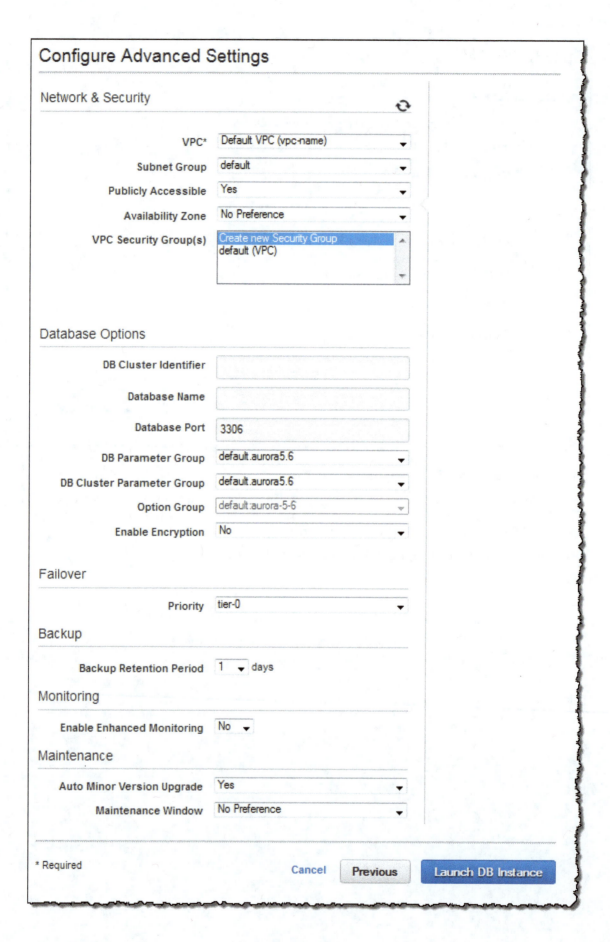

Configure Advanced Settings

Network & Security

VPC*	Default VPC (vpc-name) ▾
Subnet Group	default ▾
Publicly Accessible	Yes ▾
Availability Zone	No Preference ▾
VPC Security Group(s)	Create new Security Group / default (VPC)

Database Options

DB Cluster Identifier	
Database Name	
Database Port	3306
DB Parameter Group	default.aurora5.6 ▾
DB Cluster Parameter Group	default.aurora5.6 ▾
Option Group	default:aurora-5-6 ▾
Enable Encryption	No ▾

Failover

Priority	tier-0 ▾

Backup

Backup Retention Period	1 ▾ days

Monitoring

Enable Enhanced Monitoring	No ▾

Maintenance

Auto Minor Version Upgrade	Yes ▾
Maintenance Window	No Preference ▾

* Required   Cancel   Previous   Launch DB Instance

8. Choose **Launch DB Instance** to launch your Aurora MySQL DB instance, and then choose **Close** to close the wizard.

On the Amazon RDS console, the new DB instance appears in the list of DB instances. The DB instance has a status of **creating** until the DB instance is created and ready for use. When the state changes to **available**, you can connect to the primary instance for your DB cluster. Depending on the DB instance class and store allocated, it can take several minutes for the new instance to be available.

To view the newly created cluster, choose the **Clusters** view in the Amazon RDS console. For more information, see the Amazon RDS documentation .

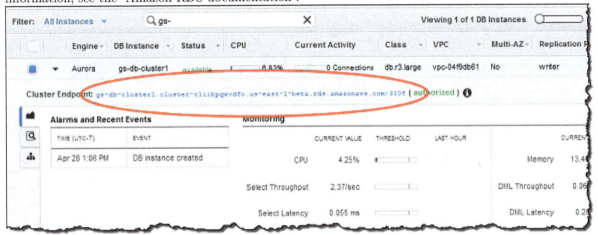

Note the port and the endpoint of the cluster. Use the endpoint and port of the cluster in your JDBC and ODBC connection strings for any application that performs write or read operations.

Migrating MySQL to Amazon Aurora MySQL by Using mysqldump

You can create a dump of your data using the `mysqldump` utility, and then import that data into an existing Amazon Aurora MySQL DB cluster.

Because Amazon Aurora MySQL is a MySQL-compatible database, you can use the `mysqldump` utility to copy data from your MySQL or MariaDB database to an existing Amazon Aurora MySQL DB cluster.

Migrating Data from an Amazon RDS MySQL DB Instance to an Amazon Aurora MySQL DB Cluster

You can migrate (copy) data to an Amazon Aurora MySQL DB cluster from an Amazon RDS snapshot, as described following.

Note
Because Amazon Aurora MySQL is compatible with MySQL, you can migrate data from your MySQL database by setting up replication between your MySQL database, and an Amazon Aurora MySQL DB cluster. We recommend that your MySQL database run MySQL version 5.5 or later.

Migrating an RDS MySQL Snapshot to Aurora MySQL

You can migrate a DB snapshot of an Amazon RDS MySQL DB instance to create an Aurora MySQL DB cluster. The new DB cluster is populated with the data from the original Amazon RDS MySQL DB instance. The DB snapshot must have been made from an Amazon RDS DB instance running MySQL 5.6.

You can migrate either a manual or automated DB snapshot. After the DB cluster is created, you can then create optional Aurora MySQL Replicas.

The general steps you must take are as follows:

1. Determine the amount of space to provision for your Amazon Aurora MySQL DB cluster. For more information, see the Amazon RDS documentation.

2. Use the console to create the snapshot in the region where the Amazon RDS MySQL 5.6 instance is located

3. If the DB snapshot is not in the region as your DB cluster, use the Amazon RDS console to copy the DB snapshot to that region. For information about copying a DB snapshot, see the Amazon RDS documentation .

4. Use the console to migrate the DB snapshot and create an Amazon Aurora MySQL DB cluster with the same databases as the original DB instance of MySQL 5.6.

Warning
Amazon RDS limits each AWS account to one snapshot copy into each region at a time.

How Much Space Do I Need?

When you migrate a snapshot of a MySQL DB instance into an Aurora MySQL DB cluster, Aurora MySQL uses an Amazon Elastic Block Store (Amazon EBS) volume to format the data from the snapshot before migrating it. In some cases, additional space is needed to format the data for migration. When migrating data into your DB cluster, observe the following guidelines and limitations:

- Although Amazon Aurora MySQL supports storage up to 64 TB in size, the process of migrating a snapshot into an Aurora MySQL DB cluster is limited by the size of the EBS volume of the snapshot. Thus, the maximum size for a snapshot that you can migrate is 6 TB.

- Tables that are not MyISAM tables and are not compressed can be up to 6 TB in size. If you have MyISAM tables, then Aurora MySQL must use additional space in the volume to convert the tables to be compatible with Aurora MySQL. If you have compressed tables, then Aurora MySQL must use additional space in the volume to expand these tables before storing them on the Aurora MySQL cluster volume. Because of this additional space requirement, you should ensure that none of the MyISAM and compressed tables being migrated from your MySQL DB instance exceeds 3 TB in size.

Reducing the Amount of Space Required to Migrate Data into Amazon Aurora MySQL

You might want to modify your database schema prior to migrating it into Amazon Aurora MySQL. Such modification can be helpful in the following cases:

- You want to speed up the migration process.

- You are unsure of how much space you need to provision.

- You have attempted to migrate your data and the migration has failed due to a lack of provisioned space.

You can make the following changes to improve the process of migrating a database into Amazon Aurora MySQL.

Important
Be sure to perform these updates on a new DB instance restored from a snapshot of a production database, rather than on a production instance. You can then migrate the data from the snapshot of your new DB instance into your Amazon Aurora MySQL DB cluster to avoid any service interruptions on your production database.

Table Type	Limitation or Guideline
MyISAM tables	Amazon Aurora MySQL supports InnoDB tables only. If you have MyISAM tables in your database, then those tables must be converted before being migrated into Amazon Aurora MySQL. The conversion process requires additional space for the MyISAM to InnoDB conversion during the migration procedure. To reduce your chances of running out of space or to speed up the migration process, convert all of your MyISAM tables to InnoDB tables before migrating them. The size of the resulting InnoDB table is equivalent to the size required by Amazon Aurora MySQL for that table. To convert a MyISAM table to InnoDB, run the following command: `alter table <schema>.<table_name> engine=innodb, algorithm=copy;`
Compressed tables	Amazon Aurora MySQL does not support compressed tables (that is, tables created with `ROW_FORMAT=COMPRESSED`). To reduce your chances of running out of space or to speed up the migration process, expand your compressed tables by setting `ROW_FORMAT` to `DEFAULT`, `COMPACT`, `DYNAMIC`, or `REDUNDANT`. For more information, see https://dev.mysql.com/doc/refman/5.6/en/innodb-row-format.html.

You can use the following SQL script on your existing MySQL DB instance to list the tables in your database that are MyISAM tables or compressed tables.

```
1. -- This script examines a MySQL database for conditions that will block
2. -- migrating the database into an Amazon Aurora MySQL DB.
3. -- It needs to be run from an account that has read permission for the
4. -- INFORMATION_SCHEMA database.
5.
```

```
6   6.  -- Verify that this is a supported version of MySQL.
7   7.
8   8.  select msg as `==> Checking current version of MySQL.`
9   9.  from
10  10.    (
11  11.    select
12  12.      'This script should be run on MySQL version 5.6. ' +
13  13.      'Earlier versions are not supported.' as msg,
14  14.      cast(substring_index(version(), '.', 1) as unsigned) * 100 +
15  15.        cast(substring_index(substring_index(version(), '.', 2), '.', -1)
16  16.        as unsigned)
17  17.      as major_minor
18  18.    ) as T
19  19.  where major_minor <> 506;
20  20.
21  21.
22  22.  -- List MyISAM and compressed tables. Include the table size.
23  23.
24  24.  select concat(TABLE_SCHEMA, '.', TABLE_NAME) as `==> MyISAM or Compressed Tables`,
25  25.  round(((data_length + index_length) / 1024 / 1024), 2) "Approx size (MB)"
26  26.  from INFORMATION_SCHEMA.TABLES
27  27.  where
28  28.    ENGINE <> 'InnoDB'
29  29.    and
30  30.    (
31  31.      -- User tables
32  32.      TABLE_SCHEMA not in ('mysql', 'performance_schema',
33  33.                             'information_schema')
34  34.      or
35  35.      -- Non-standard system tables
36  36.      (
37  37.        TABLE_SCHEMA = 'mysql' and TABLE_NAME not in
38  38.          (
39  39.            'columns_priv', 'db', 'event', 'func', 'general_log',
40  40.            'help_category', 'help_keyword', 'help_relation',
41  41.            'help_topic', 'host', 'ndb_binlog_index', 'plugin',
42  42.            'proc', 'procs_priv', 'proxies_priv', 'servers', 'slow_log',
43  43.            'tables_priv', 'time_zone', 'time_zone_leap_second',
44  44.            'time_zone_name', 'time_zone_transition',
45  45.            'time_zone_transition_type', 'user'
46  46.          )
47  47.      )
48  48.    )
49  49.    or
50  50.    (
51  51.      -- Compressed tables
52  52.        ROW_FORMAT = 'Compressed'
53  53.    );
```

The script produces output similar to the output in the following example. The example shows two tables that must be converted from MyISAM to InnoDB. The output also includes the approximate size of each table in megabytes (MB).

```
1   1.  +--------------------------------+-------------------+
2   2.  | ==> MyISAM or Compressed Tables | Approx size (MB) |
```

```
3. +----------------------------------+------------------+
4. | test.name_table                  |          2102.25 |
5. | test.my_table                    |            65.25 |
6. +----------------------------------+------------------+
7. 2 rows in set (0.01 sec)
```

Migrating a DB Snapshot by Using the Console

You can migrate a DB snapshot of an Amazon RDS MySQL DB instance to create an Aurora MySQL DB cluster. The new DB cluster will be populated with the data from the original Amazon RDS MySQL DB instance. The DB snapshot must have been made from an Amazon RDS DB instance running MySQL 5.6 and must not be encrypted. For information about creating a DB snapshot, see the Amazon RDS documentation.

If the DB snapshot is not in the AWS Region where you want to locate your data, use the Amazon RDS console to copy the DB snapshot to that region. For information about copying a DB snapshot, see the Amazon RDS documentation.

When you migrate the DB snapshot by using the console, the console takes the actions necessary to create both the DB cluster and the primary instance.

You can also choose for your new Aurora MySQL DB cluster to be encrypted "at rest" using an AWS Key Management Service (AWS KMS) encryption key. This option is available only for unencrypted DB snapshots.

To migrate a MySQL 5.6 DB snapshot by using the console

1. Sign in to the AWS Management Console and open the Amazon RDS console at https://console.aws. amazon.com/rds/.

2. Choose **Snapshots**.

3. On the **Snapshots** page, choose the snapshot that you want to migrate into an Aurora MySQL DB cluster.

4. Choose **Migrate Database**.

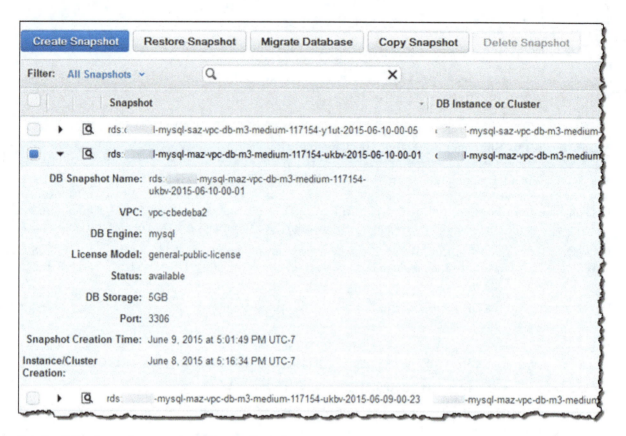

5. Set the following values on the **Migrate Database** page:

- **DB Instance Class**: Select a DB instance class that has the required storage and capacity for your database, for example `db.r3.large`. Aurora MySQL cluster volumes automatically grow as the amount of data in your database increases, up to a maximum size of 64 terabytes (TB). So you only need to select a DB instance class that meets your current storage requirements.

- **DB Instance Identifier**: Type a name for the DB cluster that is unique for your account in the region you selected. This identifier is used in the endpoint addresses for the instances in your DB cluster. You might choose to add some intelligence to the name, such as including the region and DB engine you selected, for example **aurora-cluster1**.

  The DB instance identifier has the following constraints:

  - It must contain from 1 to 63 alphanumeric characters or hyphens.
  - Its first character must be a letter.
  - It cannot end with a hyphen or contain two consecutive hyphens.
  - It must be unique for all DB instances per AWS account, per AWS Region.

- **VPC:** If you have an existing VPC, then you can use that VPC with your Amazon Aurora MySQL DB cluster by selecting your VPC identifier, for example `vpc-a464d1c1`. For information on using an existing VPC, see the Amazon RDS documentation.

  Otherwise, you can choose to have Amazon RDS create a VPC for you by selecting **Create a new VPC**.

- **Subnet Group:** If you have an existing subnet group, then you can use that subnet group with your Amazon Aurora MySQL DB cluster by selecting your subnet group identifier, for example `gs-subnet-group1`.

122

Otherwise, you can choose to have Amazon RDS create a subnet group for you by selecting **Create a new subnet group**.

- **Publicly Accessible:** Select **No** to specify that instances in your DB cluster can only be accessed by resources inside of your VPC. Select **Yes** to specify that instances in your DB cluster can be accessed by resources on the public network. The default is **Yes. Note**
Your production DB cluster might not need to be in a public subnet, because only your application servers will require access to your DB cluster. If your DB cluster doesn't need to be in a public subnet, set **Publicly Accessible** to **No**.

- **Availability Zone:** Select the Availability Zone to host the primary instance for your Aurora MySQL DB cluster. To have Amazon RDS select an Availability Zone for you, select **No Preference**.

- **Database Port:** Type the default port to be used when connecting to instances in the DB cluster. The default is 3306. **Note**
You might be behind a corporate firewall that doesn't allow access to default ports such as the MySQL default port, 3306. In this case, provide a port value that your corporate firewall allows. Remember that port value later when you connect to the Aurora MySQL DB cluster.

- **Enable Encryption:** Choose **Yes** for your new Aurora MySQL DB cluster to be encrypted "at rest." If you choose **Yes**, you will be required to choose an AWS KMS encryption key as the **Master Key** value.

- **Auto Minor Version Upgrade:** Select **Yes** if you want to enable your Aurora MySQL DB cluster to receive minor MySQL DB engine version upgrades automatically when they become available.

The **Auto Minor Version Upgrade** option only applies to upgrades to MySQL minor engine versions for your Amazon Aurora MySQL DB cluster. It doesn't apply to regular patches applied to maintain system stability.

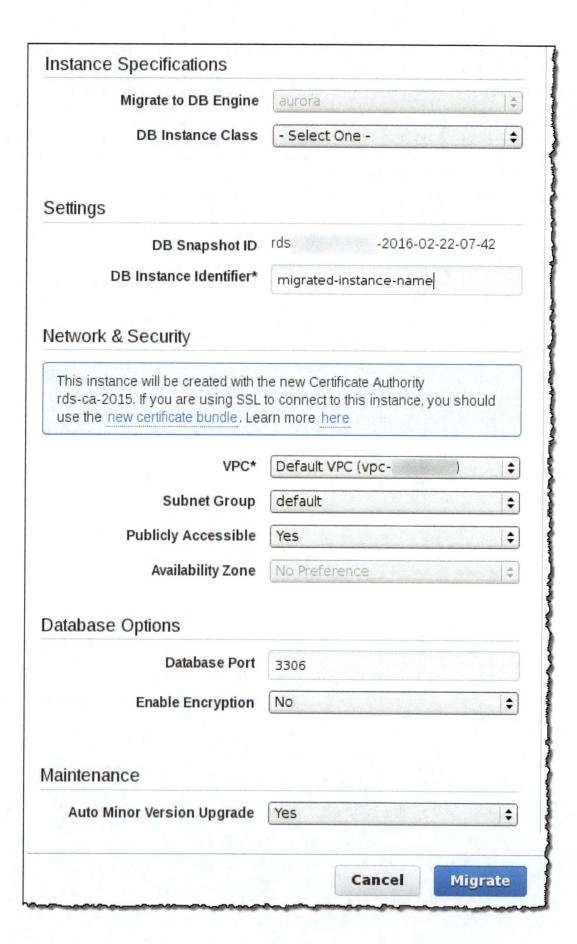

6. Choose **Migrate** to migrate your DB snapshot.

7. Choose **Instances**, and then choose the arrow icon to show the DB cluster details and monitor the progress of the migration. On the details page, you will find the cluster endpoint used to connect to the primary instance of the DB cluster. For more information on connecting to an Amazon Aurora MySQL DB cluster, see the Amazon RDS documentation.

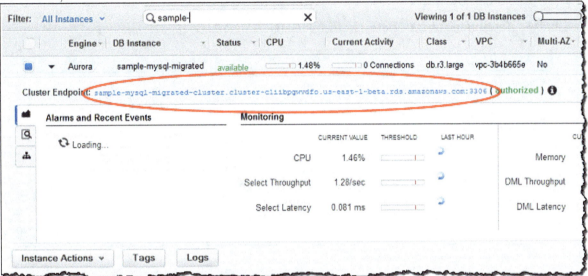

Document History

The following table describes the important changes to the documentation since the last release of AWS Database Migration Service Step-by-Step Migration Guide.

- **API version:** 20160101
- **Latest documentation update:** August 30, 2017

Change	Description	Date
Microsoft SQL Server to Aurora migration guide added	Added Microsoft SQL Server to Amazon Aurora with MySQL compatibility database migration guide.	August 30, 2017
Oracle to PostgreSQL migration guide added	Added Oracle to PostgreSQL database migration guide.	August 18, 2017
On-premises Oracle to Amazon Aurora migration guide added	Added On-premises Oracle to Amazon Aurora database migration guide.	November 17, 2016

www.ingramcontent.com/pod-product-compliance
Lightning Source LLC
LaVergne TN
LVHW082040050326
832904LV00005B/245